Too Close For Comfort

Escape from a Destructive Cult

SG Williams
BSc.(Hons) RAc.

DEDICATION

This is for Irene who encouraged me to write this story many years ago. Without her love, patience, insight and all-night talks, the ending may have been very different. I had always known Irene to be a wonderful giving person that not only helped me through my confusion, but was a support for many others.

Enjoy life.
Your learnings and thoughts are precious.
Hold them as your treasure from God.
The Lord is dealing graciously with you that your joy
may be made known to many.
For God is our strength and our salvation.
Whom shall we fear?
Peace and joy be with you.
Love Irene.

CONTENTS

CONTENTS

ACKNOWLEDGMENTS

I want to thank my mom, Marion, who has been a constant support and a sounding board. I want to thank Howard, my best friend and team-mate who has been a source of strength and an inspiration. He is someone who has an important and noticeable presence for good in this world and has inspired me to turn up the volume of my own voice through my publishing endeavours. I also want to acknowledge my first husband, who was an integral part of this story but who left us far too soon. It was he who helped me escape and gave the world our three beautiful children, who would not be here if it wasn't for him.

ACKNOWLEDGMENTS

INTRODUCTION

This is a true and disturbing account of the thoughts and mindset of an individual that loses themselves to a zealous Christian fundamentalist cult. It is closely based on real characters and true events that happened in Canada in the 1980's. Throughout the story, the names, places and locations have been changed. The story was documented in 1989 on a 5.25 inch floppy disk, first published in 2006 and republished to a wider audience in 2021. The group that is at the centre of this story, was identified and exposed as a destructive cult by the Committee on Mind Abuse (COMA) in Toronto in the 1990's. The same church is still in operation today with a branch in Canada.

The number of cult-like victims worldwide has markedly increased in recent times. Harmful influential groups and individuals are everywhere. They are on social media, among our friends and families and in our communities. They can be political, religious or business-based, driven by both greed and ideology. The key is that destructive groups are not easy to recognize and many are well disguised. The process of being converted to following the group is not obvious but works on its victim slowly and persistently as part of a subtle long term process that touches everyone in the victim's life. Nobody is immune.

Popular belief is that getting pulled in and taken advantage by a coercive organization only happens to people who are weak. Most believe this would never happen to them. However the techniques of brainwashing are well documented, effective and powerful even against those who are strong willed. The most damaging groups or individuals can be the extremist, highly visible radical groups. They are easily recognized. However many of the most successful and harmful of all, are those that appear innocuous, mimicking do-gooders that have as their agents, our loving partners, friends and family who are familiar and non-threatening. These are the groups that hide behind known traditional organizations.

We all experience subtle manipulation of alien thinking being planted in our subconscious. It is easy to get caught up in fashionable thought, opinion and caring about what others think and say about us. However, at the other end of the spectrum, is manipulation that is extreme in magnitude. There are groups who use and train their members in overt techniques of persuasion. It is one thing to kidnap someone against their will. It is an entirely different level of depravity when a well trained group, intentionally hijacks someone's mind and convinces them that they want to disappear, coercing them to do so willingly. This is the ultimate violation, mind control over another human being. Leaders of such groups do things that are brutal but yet are considered angels.

With the polarization of world politics, it is important to examine our own thinking, question long held assumptions and guard ourselves against victimization by coercive external forces. These pages contain lessons about what happens when we lose objectivity while immersing in radical thinking and bizarre beliefs. Sometimes we have blinders on and don't see the whole picture. Sometimes we fail to examine our long held beliefs because they are accepted by those around us. This tale is both a warning and a wake up call. Those that are wise will learn from adversity and only those who have the courage to examine their own life, will achieve the freedom, fulfillment and happiness we were all created for.

Daniel 12:9-10

But He said, Go now Daniel, for what I have said is not to be understood until the time of the end. Many shall be purified by great trials and persecutions. But the wicked shall continue in their wickedness, and none of them will understand. Only those willing to learn will understand what it means.

The key to breaking the hold of any extreme group or individual is understanding how the victim thinks. It helps to see examples of how mind control is applied in everyday situations. This book was written for those of you who are questioning your allegiance to a group that has sprouted some red flags. It is for those who have been a victim of a cult-like group and are looking for validation of their experience. I hope this story will ignite a light at the end of tunnel and help you see your way out. This is also for those who have lost someone to an alien belief system and want to get them back. I pray that those who have already lost someone to brainwashing, will find hope.

- SG Williams - June 27, 2021

CHAPTER ONE

In all of this massive city, I just happened to choose the same corner of Main Street as Grant who was standing there idling watching the crowds of people pass by. This throughway stretched miles from one end of this metropolis to the other. I was handing out pamphlets of Christian literature with the naivety and zeal of my new found faith. Grant was amusing himself at the expense of a number of Hare Krishna followers that had set up shop nearby. He was eyeing the shaved heads, ponytails and salmon pink pyjamas, as curiously as I was. Now looking back at that day, I wonder if Grant thought that our little group of Christian zealots was just as odd, as the ensemble of men in their strange uniforms, playing their tambourines.

I certainly never imagined being a part of a radical religious organization on a crusade to save the world. I had never even thought about living this far from my home, just one hour outside one of the country's largest cities. I had arrived here as a transfer student to complete the last couple of years of my Honours degree. That summer before I arrived I stayed at home with my parents while I worked at our local university. It was at this research institution that I became friends with a coworker named Ross. Ross drove with me halfway across the country so I could attend this new university.

My new residence seemed so far away. It was a long drive especially when Ross was driving. Even though I tried to get some rest when he was behind the wheel, I was constantly jerked wide awake with every grind of the gears. I had just taught him to drive my new silver pinstriped Datsun 200sx with a standard transmission. He had only ever driven an automatic car and he struggled with the manual drive. This was the first time I had travelled this far home inside my own country. During high school I had travelled to Europe twice and had visited five countries, but exploration of my larger home had just begun. I had always wanted to visit the Big City and I was excited about the prospect of living just one hour away.

This new university town would not be one hundred percent new territory. There would be other people from my home university that I knew, who had also transferred here to finish their degree programs. However I had already promised myself that I was not going to get involved with this same crowd. I wanted a fresh start and wanted to meet some new friends. Many of the friends I acquired in the past, just happened to come into my path. I had never gone out of my way to make friends and never really felt a need to. They had either befriended me or just occurred naturally because of a common interest. This time I wanted to shape my own social circle and make friends with people I really wanted to be friends with.

At my home town college, I had many acquaintances. I knew a lot of people. I spent a lot of time studying and partied anonymously and with whomever. This was easy to do because the college was very small and everyone knew each other. When I graduated with a Laboratory Technology Diploma, I felt very proud that I had received

High Honours and had made the Principal's List. However during the anticlimax, I couldn't help but look back and wonder about all the good times and good memories. There weren't any really. My studies had been so important that I hadn't made much effort to make friends and even less to keep them. This time things were going to be different. This time I wanted to enjoy myself and not just focus on my grades.

Ross and I arrived at my new university in mid afternoon after a bout of hair raising car trouble during the Big City's noon traffic, on the four lane trans-country highway. After a number of wrong exits, wrong turns and wrestling with the map, we found my future home in East Residence. This was a very large coed residence with sixteen hundred students and three cafeterias under one roof. I had a single room because I was a third year, mature student. The room was located on the fourth floor of one of the cement and brick towers with a little balcony overlooking one of the internal grassy courtyards. It was called the Atlantic Tower.

Ross helped me get settled into my little room. I was getting anxious to explore the university. I had wanted to attend the orientation events because I was afraid there was something or some information I might miss. However Ross reminded me that this was his vacation and I could find out whatever I needed later. I balked at first and then recalled what orientation was really about. How could I forget what had happened at the college back home and the humiliation the older students inflicted on the freshmen, fuelled by the previous year's revenge. No thank you, I had enough of that in my early university years.

I decided I was not interested in that I could survive without knowing all the words to our residence cheer. However I did experience one mishap as the result of orientation. One evening, as I was walking from the massive exposed parking area, surrounded by fields of lawn facing the entrance to East Residence, I spotted a tractor a long way off, towing a wagon full of women. I saw them looking in my direction but was not sure why. Then a couple of guys in jeans jumped off the tractor and started jogging towards me. I was the only person around and they were pointing at me. I started running for the door but just as I grabbed the handle they grabbed me.

No amount of protest would stop them. I had planned to register for my classes early that evening because Ross and I had plans. I was a little bit angry because I was placed on the party wagon and not allowed off. I was made a prisoner and was taken a long way from my residence to a wooded area behind some barns. Once there I was let go and a beer was placed in my hands. There was already a large party going on around a huge bonfire and music was playing. I did not know a single soul there and had no idea where I was. I stayed for one beer and then just before dark, was able to find my way back to residence.

As soon as we could, Ross and I headed out on our vacation to see the sites and explore this part of the country. There was a lot to see in the Big City and this was a treat for the both of us. We even visited his brother and his brother's wife, who was pregnant with their first child. We only had a week to travel. Ross left just before the routine of classes descended on me. A few months went by and I had to remind myself about Ross. Instead of the old saying "Absence makes the heart grow fonder", I found more truth in the ole "Out of sight, out of mind".

This university, made up of a collection of old colleges, was situated in a beautiful setting and had a lot to offer besides academia. The campus itself was a patchwork of wide open spaces, green lawns and well groomed trees frequented by large aggressive black squirrels. A mix of old and new architectural structures inhabited the high density central campus. The buildings in this area were separated by brick and concrete walkways with stairs and large landing areas lined with benches and gardens. These cement pathways wandered in all directions to more remote destinations with an arboretum in the north and farm land with barns and animals in the south. The residences were mostly to the east with a golf course and rolling hills in the west. The older pathways in particular reminded me of the yellow brick road from the Wizard of Oz.

Within a very short period of time I met and became friends with Kathy. We sat near each other in the Atlantic cafeteria near the tower I lived in. We recognized each other from the college back home. Kathy had transferred in the previous year and although we knew who the other was, we had never spoken before until now. We both lived in the Atlantic section of the residence but I was in Tower Two and she was in Tower Three. Because she was close by, I started visiting her for tea in the evenings. Through Kathy, I met a whole new group of other students. The five of us began to form strong bonds and socialized together at functions. Together we went to dances, restaurants on campus and movies like the Rocky Horror Picture Show.

Kathy and Ann were friends since the previous year. Kathy was in the last year of the same program I was in. Ann was in Landscape Architecture. She was friends with a classmate by the name of Greg who was also in her landscape program. Ann was very serious and had an acute social conscience. Her best friend from home was just across town in the Jesuit college. Greg was a cowboy from a large ranch in the prairies. He liked to wear his Stetson and calf high boots and I thought it was just his style until I realized that his family raised cattle on a huge expanse of land. He was a real cowboy. His friend Doug was a city dweller. All of us lived in Towers Two and Three in close proximity to one another.

At the same time I also became closer friends with two of my classmates from the college back home. We were in the same year of our program, transferred together and shared most of the same classes. Tom, Pam and I often met after classes to work on assignments and get help from one another. Pam was even more studious than I was. She was always the person to go to for any questions or clarification. She kept a better track of when assignments were due and what tests or exams were looming, than I did. True to my promise to myself, I was trying to loosen up a bit while keeping A grades. I was not looking for A+s this time or an honours standing. Tom struggled a bit more than Pam and I did. He would come to me first for help or questions and to Pam when I was not available. Tom and I were close friends before and now, more so.

CHAPTER TWO

Then there was Kari and Beth who showed up at my door one evening unannounced. They were responding to information I have given them in a survey. I had completely forgotten about the survey until they showed it to me. I remembered being stopped by people outside the gymnasium after I finished registering for classes. A university club had set up a table and I just thought this was part of the registration process and information dissemination. Beth handed me a little orange coloured sheet of paper with my name and address on campus, that I had completed at registration. The questions asked about my belief in God, religious affiliations, my knowledge of the *Bible* and if I was interested in participating in a Bible Study.

Ross and I had often discussed religion. His family heritage was Polish and they were very serious about their religion. He once told me that a person could not truly be a Christian unless they were Catholic. I did not agree and we argued about that off and on. However neither one of us had much knowledge on the subject or had studied the *Bible*. Our discussions were largely based on opinion. I had vowed someday to prove him wrong. My new university had sent an orientation package to my home before I moved here. Information about a Bible Study group was advertised and I had decided even before I arrived at the university, I would join. I wanted to learn enough to prove Ross wrong. With little further thought on that subject I filled out the survey about religion that day at the gymnasium and checked "yes" about joining a Bible Study.

I slowly remembered all of this as Kari and Beth stood at my door in Atlantic Tower. I began feeling apprehensive however. I hesitantly invited them in to talk more and felt guarded as if ready to fend off an attempt to convert me to their brand of religion. I was upfront and clear with them to the point of being rude. I explained that I wanted to learn about the *Bible* but that I would interpret the scripture for myself. I was not interested in conforming to someone else's views and opinions on the matter. I had dug my heels in on this because for me, this was a continuation of my arguments with Ross.

Kari was persistent however in reviewing a little booklet she had brought to share with me despite my lack of receptivity. I was not interested in being fed information about religion or scripture. I had been very argumentative in this subject area for quite some time now. I had met too many people with conflicting views. Every one of them believed he or she was the sole bearer of the truth and that all others were wrong. I was not interested in one more version of the so-called truth to add to the confusion. I made a final protest by saying, "I don't want other people telling me what to believe", and then I let Kari and Beth run through their little prepared speech.

As they spoke they pointed to little pictures in the booklet and quoted the scripture written on the bottom of each page. The first diagram showed a benevolent looking old man explaining how God loved each one of us and that

20

we were specially created to fulfill a plan He had for us. Secondly, a depiction of an angry person helped illustrate the message that all of us have sinned and have become separated from God. The third page said that because God is holy and just and our sins are deserving of punishment and in that eternal separation we were destined to go to hell. Then the following page outlined a cross as a bridge joining two landmasses with a canyon in the middle. They explained how Jesus, who is divine and loves us, took on that eternal condemnation we deserved. On our behalf, He paid that debt as a holy sacrifice of His death, through His crucifixion on the cross. That Jesus is the bridge that crosses over that chasm pit of hell, so we can be reunited with God. The last page was a call to action. We must admit we have sins, ask for God's forgiveness and accept Christ's payment for us so we can have the relationship with God that He intended.

This was a very simple children's version of a Christian message. At the same time they described some very deep and profound ideas. I was disarmed because I really did not know enough to argue with them. I had never heard this message delivered in this way before. Instead I asked them to explain some of the concepts in more detail hoping to see the flaw in their reasoning or move to ground I knew something about. These women were not fazed by my detailed interrogation and it soon became evident that they knew a lot about the *Bible* and scripture. I was impressed. They left a number of verses for me to look up for myself and suggested that to start reading the *Bible*, it was better to start in the *New Testament* with *John*. Reading from the beginning in *Genesis* can be difficult.

I was still quite uncomfortable with Kari and Beth. However my level of curiosity had overcome my caution. Before I realized what I was agreeing to, I consented to holding a Bible Study in my room. Afterwards I realized that by having the study here, in my room, I could not skip

21

out. I was relieved when they finally left. I did not want anyone to see me with them and question me about who they were. I was embarrassed and did not want anyone to know about my looming Bible Study either.

All my friends lived in the East Residence. We never had to leave the building to visit one another. Most weeknights I would study until ten or ten thirty and then drop into Kathy's place for tea. This was a very traditional thing for people from home to do. Other times I would visit Pam or Tom, especially if I had questions about course work. I liked getting out of my room for a change of scenery and looked forward to visiting my friends. I also enjoyed going to the pubs but preferred good conversation and a cup of tea even more. Plus on a student budget, staying in was more prudent financially, as well as academically. I still wanted to get good grades but not break my back to get great grades. I felt I had finally found that balance I was looking for.

I was not the only one to gravitate to Kathy's place. Most of the others would eventually end up there too. When everyone showed up, there were seven of us. Some curled up on the bed, the rest would sit on the floor or in the one chair. We were all older than the average student and considered ourselves mature. Most of us were from back home and others would laugh at our little tea parties. We said that as old fashioned as it seemed, we were just expressing our heritage. At home, as soon as the company arrived, a pot of tea would be placed on the stove to brew if it had not already been topped up after steeping all day.

Tom, Pam and myself saw each other continuously because we were in the same classes, majoring in the same program as we were in the same year. The university population had a special name for us because of our program. We also had another specific handle because of the geographic region of origin. We were Eggies, who had

22

a reputation on campus for leadership abilities and high levels of involvement in extracurricular activities. Among the Eggies were us Boggers who were famous for their devoted partying and drinking. The stereotype was well known and came about by a few outstanding students from our home college that had been to this university in previous years.

Those I associated with did have some to the attributes us Boggers were labelled with. I certainly enjoyed drinking beer and dancing my heart out at the Bullring on Thursday nights. The Bullring was a place where anything was acceptable. I also frequented a number of parties that sprung up on campus. There were parties for all occasions. When the American hostages were freed from Iran I went to a party to celebrate that. People even showed up in costumes dressed on yellow ribbons, as terrorists and sheiks.

The frequency of my evenings of fun and entertainment began to diminish with the increase in visits from Kari and Beth. They always arrived unexpectedly and without invitation just when I was getting ready to go out with my friends. Even though I had expressed my plans, we would start talking about something and before I realized it, it was too late to go out. More and more of my time with my friends was being replaced with these visits and conversations with Kari and Beth. They were nice people and I did enjoy talking to them so I found it hard to turn them away.

Beth had a great sense of humour and could find comedy in almost anything. Kari was more quiet and reserved but smiled a lot. She was short and plump and although she did not have the figure of an athlete, she was. Beth was an extrovert and self confident with long wavy hair that always looked like she had been in a windstorm. Her hair was wild and natural, her face and hands were

23

tanned and she appeared to glow with health and vitality. Both were always plainly dressed donning canvas shoulder bags filled with *Bibles* and pamphlets. Neither wore makeup which made them seem younger than they were. Both were in their late twenties while I had just turned twenty three.

These women were extremely thoughtful and considerate. They remembered all my life details, everything I mentioned or told them about myself and they seemed sincerely interested in me as a person. They were forever baking homemade muffins and delivering them just in time to wish me luck on a test or exam. I felt a little overwhelmed by their concern and attention and could not find a way to return the kindness they had shown me. I had been very cold to Kari and Beth when they first came to my door. However something had happened to me before that first visit and the first scheduled Bible Study in my room, that changed my attitude towards them. It made me want to hear what they had to say and get to know them a little better.

CHAPTER THREE

I re-read the little pamphlet that Kari and Beth reviewed on their first visit. It was called *The Five Spiritual Absolutes*. Initially I just skimmed over it and was not particularly interested. I did decide however to take their advice about reading the *Bible*. I had attempted it a few times before. It was a classic that really should be read, after all. Plus there was so much controversy surrounding the content in those pages and because I found myself, of late, engaging in religious discussions, I could not voice an educated opinion unless I had studied it for myself.

On previous occasions I struggled through *Genesis, Leviticus* and then came to a complete halt in *Numbers*. Beth had suggested that I start by reading *John* in the *New Testament*. It had never occurred to me to not start at the beginning. After supper, just a week after that first visit from Kari and Beth, I opened the New American Standard version of the *Bible* that these women had left with me on loan. The first thing I noticed was that the language was far easier to read than the old King James version I had been using. Next I started by reading the first fourteen verses of John.

John 1: 1-14 (NAS)

In the beginning was the Word, and the Word was with God and the Word was God. All things came into being by Him, and apart from Him nothing came into being that has come into being. In Him was life, and the Life was the light of men. And the Light shines in the darkness, and the darkness did not comprehend it.

There was a man sent by God whose name was John. He came for a witness that he might bear witness of the light that all might believe through him. He was not the light, but came that he might bear witness of the light.

There was the true Light which came into the world, enlightens every man. He was in the world and the world was made through Him and the world did not know Him. He came to His own and those that were His own did not receive Him.

But as many as received Him, to them He gave the right to become children of God, even those who believed in His name, who were not born of blood, nor the will of the flesh, nor the will of man, but of God.

And the Word became flesh, and dwelt among us, and we beheld His glory, glory as of the only begotten from the Father, full of grace and truth.

As I read, an image of Christ with a long reddish beard and hair, a long white robe and outstretched hands formed in my head as I read these verses. He was directly in front of me floating as I looked at him with arms to the side, palms up welcoming me. He spoke to me saying "I am God". I was astounded by this revelation. I did not understand that He and God were the same. I guess throughout my years of Sunday school, I had not really understood that profound detail. Knowing Jesus was Divine, for me, was the key that sort of put everything I had known into a new perspective. It was like everything I ever knew at that moment just congealed. Everything became crystal clear and solid even though I wasn't aware that any cloudiness of confusion had existed prior to that.

In that instant I understood who Jesus was and my whole life up to that point came into focus. In my mind's eye, like a video replay of my life, the reason for each past event now made sense to me as if it had been explained to me without words. All the Christian theology I had ever learned as a child in Sunday school was brought to my mind and I now understood the big picture. My life now seemed to make sense and have a purpose in the scenario before me. Even though I could never verbalize or explain the details, I experienced an all knowing and complete understanding of all things and the entire world in that vision of Christ.

When I came to my senses, I was so overwhelmed that I just sat on the side of my bed with my mouth wide open, jaw dropped to the floor. I knew I had a choice to make and pictured myself standing at the crossroad of two paths. I could either reject what I just experienced as some bizarre mental aberration or as something real and true. My heart was convinced of the truth of God answering a long forgotten prayer, to make himself known to me. However I knew that if I choose to believe in Christ, in all aspects of my life, He would be my Lord and that my life would have to change. I saw this path as being the most difficult one. However I felt and I was privileged to experience this profound and wonderful gift. I could not just walk away from it. I prayed for forgiveness and chose Christ.

I became very aware of spiritual things and the reality of another whole world had opened up to me. I seemed to be able to see more clearly which added a whole new dimension to my life. Nothing was ordinary, everything was more than it seemed and coincidences were no longer just that. My body reacted as if I had seen a ghost and mixed with that awe, was also fear. At that time the only analogy I could think of was, as a child worrying about dragons and fairies and then years later finding out that they were real. They had been there all along despite what I had been told and what I believed as an adult. Now I realized, in retrospect, they call this an awakening. I can see why it is called that because it is as if I had been sleepwalking through life until this happened.

The fear was real but so was the immense joy and peace. When I saw my past life pass before me, I was ashamed of all the not so nice and a couple of terrible things I had done. When I asked for forgiveness, Christ showed me that the slate had been wiped clean and my relationship with God was good again. The communication was telepathic-like as I looked at that image of Jesus. I had been relieved of a large burden I didn't know I was carrying. I was not feeling sad, depressed or guilty. I thought I was a pretty good person. However when facing the All Knowing, all the facades, justifications and false ego just melted away. Who had I been fooling? When you face the Almighty, all that foolishness is stripped away and there is no choice but to get real with yourself. Now I knew I was healed and had a profound sense of wellbeing, I did not know, could ever be achieved.

I never told anyone about what happened to me that day. I was very self conscious about being labelled a religious fanatic. I was embarrassed about it in some ways. I was no longer the same person and I did not know what to do or say. However it did push me toward getting to know Kari and Beth, even though they had nothing to do with my conversion. That came from God. I knew He had heard my prayer while sliding along the Interstate, in the middle of a motorcycle accident, thinking I was going to die, a year before. I prayed to live and asked Him, "God if you are really there, show me who You are". My conversion was from God alone, but He did use Kari and Beth to encourage me to take the next step, just as he sent Ross into my life to challenge me about my beliefs. These women had a wealth of knowledge and I wanted to learn

28

more.

Whenever these women dropped by they would talk about Christ, faith and scripture. I stopped discouraging the visits and they could see that I was now interested in what they had to say. I was listening now, carefully trying to digest their ideas slowly and thoughtfully. I did not have the knowledge or experience in these matters, to argue my own position or feelings. Neither did I have any previous training on interpretation and application. I did not know how I was supposed to live according to the *Bible*. I still wanted to be cautious of what they were teaching. I was struggling to find a way to know when they were right and when I was being misled. I was hoping I would just know somehow. Although I was all in with my faith, I did so with a large dose of skepticism about what was being taught by this group.

My friendship with Kari and Beth was not a natural one. They more or less forced themselves into my life. I had already settled in with my group of seven, university friends. However I genuinely liked these women who I saw as older role models. I became quite fond of them and looked forward to seeing them. They had busy social lives in the church and were always ready to include me in their plans, even altering their schedules around my classes and commitments. They enjoyed organizing hikes and camping trips. Kari was a cross country ski instructor and taught classes on campus. One weekend the three of us piled into Beth's little sky blue Volkswagen Bug to purchase my first set of skis. After that I spent every weekend exploring local cross country trails with Kari and Beth.

I wasn't so sure I was going to enjoy cross country skiing after my first trip to the conservation area, a few miles south of the university. The trails were beautifully cut through massive stands of mature cedar. The only cedar trees I had ever seen back home consisted of small ornamental shrubs. There were many low rolling hills that made the trek a bit more challenging for a beginner. I spent a lot of time sliding back down the hills I was trying to mount. Kari also decided that we would go bushwhacking by creating new tracks through the wooded areas. It seemed to me that I had managed to wrap myself around every small tree I encountered. I was so weak from laughter, I ended up crawling back to the standard trail on my hands and knees with skis in tow. It took a few more trips after that, before I could remain upright and keep pace with Kari and Beth. I loved the challenge.

It was on these weekend excursions that I began to meet other members of their church, University Bible School (UBS). I also began to meet a lot of new people from many of the other Christian groups on campus. They all knew one another. Later I realized that this was an exclusive circle by invitation only. These networks would never be visible to the general public. Unless you were introduced as a Christian by someone in one of these groups, you would never know this sub-culture existed. Unless they were evangelizing, the members of these groups never discussed their faith with non-believers. These discussions and identities of the network, its members and activities, were only discussed with like-minded individuals who knew their language and lingo. For the most part many were not friendly with the outsiders.

Now that I had been accepted into a whole new underworld. Yet I remained cautious, watching and biting my tongue. Even though I had begun to trust Kari and Beth, I still was not comfortable around these Christians. Many of them lived in what I observed as a bubble of narrow thinking within the safety and privilege of sheltered lives. Many had never done the kind of things that would be considered normal for kids growing up in my world, which was also somewhat sheltered. But I felt these folks lived an ultra conservative limited lifestyle. Heidi was one of these people. She was a member of another group Bible Study led by Kari and Beth. She too was a student like myself living in East Residence. We met up and had lunch in one of our cafeterias one day. Following that, she came looking for me in my room. I had mentioned that she should drop by sometime but I had lied. I did not really mean it.

I was embarrassed when Heidi showed up at my door one evening. She was tall, heavy set with long straight hair parted in the middle. She had a very young face with large glasses that kept falling off her nose. She was a very nice and pleasant person but seemed very naive and innocent. I had pegged her as a goodie-goodie and was not particularly interested in being friends with her. I already had my group of seven regular friends with Kari and Beth as my Christian friends. So far, I managed to keep those two worlds separate. I had my party friends and my religious friends and did not know how Heidi would fit in. She was confusing me and messing up my little segregated world.

Heidi was not my type anyway. That evening, at my door. she caught me off guard. I was a little ticked off and my words were sharp and brief. I told her I had a lot of homework to do but she stayed anyway and we talked for longer than I wanted. We talked about our faith but I kept looking out the door, worried that my other friends would show up and hear what we were talking about. I did not want them to know about this new part of my life. Heidi did not take offence or even notice my rudeness that night and continued showing up again and again. I did not have the heart to hurt her feelings. Over time I started to like her and enjoy her visits.

Heidi often attended the non-denominational church services held on campus by UBS. This was the church group Kari and Beth belonged to. I had refused to go up until this point. However, because of Heidi, who was not connected to that church in any way besides being a student like myself, I decided to go with her. Heidi had been a long time Christian raised in a traditional church, if she was OK with this group, I felt more reassured. I felt I could trust her judgment. Kari and Beth had just been so keen on pursuing my friendship and their dedication to that end only prolonged my suspicions about their church. It just did not feel right, but over and over again, I was left with no rational explanation or proof that could support my mistrust.

The UBS church service was held in the large sloping lecture auditorium of the Arts Building, across from the massive, four floored, glass-walled library. The building that housed this theatre was an older stone structure. We had to descend a series of stairs to get to the basement. There were approximately forty adults sitting and milling around near the front, closest to the podium. We chose to move upward to the back a bit away from the others. It seems that Heidi only knew Kari and Beth from her Bible Study the same as myself.

Everyone was casually dressed with some being so casual to the point of looking a bit scruffy and tattered. I got the impression that these folks were nature loving hippy or Bohemian types. Many donned well worn blue jeans, carried canvas bags and the women wore no makeup and scarves covering their long hair, ponytails or braids. The unusually well behaved children were everywhere. These folks seemed to know each other well and were relatively young ranging from student age to thirty five. All but a few of the children were under the age of ten.

The service started as a number of people gathered at the very front. One man seemed to be in charge while the others were there in supporting roles. The man in charge, the minister I expected, opened with a prayer. The others put the words to songs up on an overhead projector and led us in the singing. There were no musical instruments and the lyrics were taken from *Bible* verses. The songs were sung with great enthusiasm with specific parts for men and women who would alternate with each verse. Most knew the songs by heart and seemed to be having fun with this. When the singing was done, the minister made some announcements and then introduced the sermon.

As if on queue, people read notebooks, readied their writing utensils and opened their *Bibles*. The sermon was more like a lecture rather than a homily. It was a Bible Study combined with an interpretation, an analysis plus an admonishment in how to behave. I found out the sermon was actually what they call Teachings. They were tough, no nonsense approaches to living. It was clear that the minister had no fear of offending anyone. Although my first impression was a good one, I thought there was something odd about this group. Other than the plainness of dress, the quiet children, the over the top friendliness and more than usual prevalence of happiness, I just could not put my finger on it. The service was more than one and a half hours long. The children were just too complacent. The adults were just too happy. I again wondered if it was a cult.

However I continued to go. I thought the Teachings were excellent. What better way to obtain the knowledge I was seeking. I could still read the scripture for myself and take my own interpretation in the end. That was what I had planned to do. The amount of Biblical ground covered by this group was tremendous. My awakening experience left me thirsty to find out who Jesus was, who God was and what they expected from me. After all, these were no longer just mythological characters. In my new world, I felt the weight of responsibility to do what is right given my new found belief. Whatever that was.

In subsequent Teachings I noticed that there were three

33

men who took turns delivering the message for that week. These teachers were called Elders and there were three of them that were in charge of the UBS church. There was not one minister and I was not sure if these men had the same credentials as a traditional minister. Ron worked as a full time Elder and at that time, had two children. He was short with dark hair, a moustache and a loud commanding voice. He had an inflection to his voice that reminded me of the born-again southern healing preachers you see on TV sometimes. He had a strong command of scripture and was an excellent teacher although sometimes I felt his personality was more suited to that of a used car salesman. I just did not trust him and it took years for me to find out why.

One of the other Elders was named Jeff. He was very tall, humble and soft spoken. He had advanced graduate degrees, was very quiet and rarely spoke. However he was very powerful within the UBS church and everyone listened when he did speak. He was eloquent, passionate and had an authoritative voice. He had a wide mouth bracketed by large dimples. He always wore jeans and stooped a bit when he walked. Jeff was single and I liked him the best. He seemed approachable but always unavailable. He was not easy to corner and after a few attempts to connect with him, I was left feeling he was not the person he appeared to be. Perhaps the feigned shyness was actually aloofness, pride. He was definitely avoiding me and I felt he was judging me somehow. .

The third Elder, Brian, was a less imposing figure. He did not teach as well as the other two, in my opinion. He did not have the same clarity of thought, depth of understanding and experience. He was the newest of the Elders. He was a car mechanic by trade and did that work part-time. Brian, like Ron, was married but had only one child. He often repaired the cars of church members. He and Ron were not available like Jeff who was single and did not spend as much time socializing with the church members. Each Elder also had jurisdiction over parts of the community and the geographic area of the town. Ron and Brian spent more time with the married couples and children, situated off campus. Jeff however lived close to campus property, ran a household of male students and hosted all the extra-curricular church activities for the singles.

The University Bible School (UBS) was listed at the university as a club and maintained club status as a student organization in 1980. It was affiliated with an international group of churches known by many different names, located on numerous campuses in the United States and other countries. In order for this church to qualify as a student club, it had to have a set percentage of students as members. One Sunday the Elders passed around a sheet of paper to collect the signature of students to maintain that status. This church benefited greatly by operating as a student club. It did not need to fund a separate building, and could use the campus buildings, free of charge for events. UBS also had access to a large population of pliable and open minds as prospective members, to increase their ranks.

The formal proliferation of their belief system was by means of the Teachings delivered at its regular Sunday service offerings. In addition there were special scheduled meetings for various purposes, weekly Bible Study and classes about other religions every week. Sunday nights were for fellowship at the Breaking of Bread. Here was an opportunity for more informal lessons with prayer and scripture reading by everyone in the circle followed by a potluck supper. Everyone contributed but the non-students were expected to take the lion's share of the load to serve and feed the participating students. I found that the most valuable knowledge was what I gleaned from listening to the private discussions between the groups of friends.

35

These Christians spent most of their time, outside of work or school, with each other and they mostly talked about their faith experiences.

CHAPTER FOUR

My primary group of friends through my first fall and winter semester, continued to be the group I met at Kathy's evening tea parties, plus my classmates Tom and Pam. These were my regular friends not affiliated with a religious group. The only church activity I attended regularly was the Bible Study that was held in my room. Most of what I was learning about Christianity came from my continued readings of the *Bible*, on my own and conversations with Kari and Beth.

When everyone arrived at my room for that first Bible Study with Kari and Beth, I was shocked when Ann showed up. Ann was one of my group of seven friends from Kathy's. Ann was also surprised and thought she had come to the wrong room, in error. I was embarrassed. I did not want any of my regular friends knowing about the Bible Study. I wanted to keep this world a secret. I was also confused and did not think Ann was religious.

Ann was a very serious woman. She was small in stature with braces, straight, fine, short, light-coloured hair that was mousy in appearance. She was very much an intellectual and a political activist who was always well informed on world events. Me, not so much. I was nervous around her. If I was careless in what I said and had not totally explored my opinion carefully, Ann would find fault, pounce on me and vigorously challenge me. She had a soft and quiet voice but her words packed a punch. I soon learned to think before I spoke or else I would end up on the defensive.

Ann did not like people who appeared inconsistent in their convictions, or had not developed them well enough. I found her refreshing to be around and although we were around the same age, I looked up to her. Through her and some of her other friends, I was introduced to social action groups like Amnesty International and other students from around the world staying at the International residences on campus. Because of Ann, I started to develop a more sensitive social conscience and pay more attention to the injustices in our world.

After that first Bible Study in my room, we talked and shared our disbelief in misjudging the other. She was even more shocked to see me at the study than I was to see her. We ended up having a good laugh about it. Ann was a Roman Catholic and was interested in learning about the *Bible* and how it applied to her Catholic faith. Her best friend from home was just across town at another college, studying to become a Priest. She often discussed theology with this friend. That inspired her to learn more about the *Bible* and afterwards often discussed what they talked about with me.

Now that I had a regular friend with an interest in religious matters. The boundaries of my two separate worlds started to collide. Because of our common interest, Ann and I started to talk about religion when we had tea at Kathy's. Kathy once told me her father was well versed in scripture, so I asked her advice and sought her opinion on a number of topics. I was very hesitant to mention

Christianity to anyone I did not know. I would never say anything if the whole crowd was there, especially if the guys were there.

However word got out and Doug started teasing some of us about being religious. He was a microbiologist and an A+ student, who loved adventure as much as he did his studies. He and Greg were both Dungeon and Dragon enthusiasts. Doug never did anything half-hearted and his exuberant criticism of religion of any kind, was consistent with his personality. Doug began teasing us when he found out that Ann and myself were taking Bible Study classes.

I found out that Ann and Kathy had been sharing their religious interests with each other for some time. They had been leaving me out of the conversation until now. They too were careful who they talked to. However, now, we started sharing our religious interests more and this became a topic of conversation, when only the three of us showed up for the nightly tea party. These discussions tweaked Kathy's interest in learning more. Soon, she too started attending the Bible Study in my room with Kari, Beth, Ann, myself and recently Heidi.

Our group of seven had developed an underground information system of sharing what we had learned. My classmate Pam had also been talking to Kathy about religion. However none of us wanted to talk openly with the whole group with all of the seven present. Everyone was afraid of being judged and harassed by Doug, Greg and Tom, but especially Doug. Nobody wanted to be singled out and made the butt of Doug's jokes. However before the Christmas break, Pam also joined our Bible Study. Of my group of seven regular friends, now all but three were involved in the Bible Study and the four of us had all been deemed too religious for Doug's liking.

The first of the winter semester, of the following year,

felt very different for me. I spent most of my time with my religious friends who attended my Bible Study. I missed the crowd at Kathy's. Everyone seemed to be more focused on the course work and many of us had vowed not to fall behind like we did last semester. The Bible Study soon became the mechanism by which we kept in touch on a regular basis. I still saw Doug and Greg on occasion and eventually those friendships fell apart as Kathy's nightly tea parties were replaced by the weekly Bible Study. My classmate Tom became my only friend not involved in religion or connected with the Bible Study or UBS in any way.

Although I had started regularly attending the UBS services on Sunday, I was not interested in becoming overly involved. This campus church had a full schedule of activities that winter but my classes were very demanding. In addition to the Sunday morning Teaching, there was the Breaking of Bread and prayer Sunday afternoon, Tuesday night Bible Study at my place, Thursday night classes on other religions and a Friday night sports night. I had already committed myself to the Bible Study which was how I kept in contact will all my friends except Tom. Those friends included Kari and Beth who led the study, Heidi who I met in the cafeteria a while back, plus my original student friends Kathy, Ann and Pam. This semester I added one more activity by occasionally attending the Breaking of Bread and prayer on Sunday night.

The Breaking of Bread was a communion event held in three locations across town. I attended the one led by the Elder Jeff because it was in a house right on the edge of the campus, not far from the centre of campus and my residence. There were a total of five male members of UBS living there, Jeff and four others. They called themselves Brothers even though they were not related. The flat was accessed by a long narrow stairwell that went up three floors to the top level. The apartment was in an older house with old bare, yellowing hardwood floors. There were patches of green carpeting strategically placed over patches of the dark wood. The furnishings were sparse and well worn providing just the basic necessities. The four younger men who were students, slept in bunk beds in two of the three bedrooms. The walls were covered with religious posters. The one I remembered the most had a picture of Jesus and a list of the names He is known by, Lord of Lords, Prince of Peace, the Messiah, the Good Shepherd , King of Kings, Son of God, the Light of the World and others.

At the first meeting I discovered there was a potluck meal. I asked why I was not told and Kari told me that the regulars were expected to bring something but the students were not. All the dishes were placed on the small kitchen table and everyone helped themselves after the grace was said. The plates of food were consumed in the living room wherever you could find a place to sit. The room was very crowded and the youngest of us all sat cross legged on the floor. Everyone chatted with each other in a friendly manner but not everyone knew each other. I sat with Kari and Beth because none of my other friends had come. They were just too busy. I myself felt a little pressed for time and wondered how long all this would take.

When most people had finished eating, a small group of people quickly attended to the clean up and dish washing. The others began to take their places in a big circle around the room and the confusion of the meal time chatter started to dissipate. The women began tying scarves on their heads to cover their hair and the children drew closer to their parents' feet in little clumps on the floor. Many started opening *Bibles*, silently reading and praying with heads bowed. When the last person had settled into their spot, music sheets were passed out to the newcomers like myself.

The following forty-five minutes consisted of song, prayer and scripture readings. *Bible* verses were read aloud and expounded upon by anyone who was inspired to do so as each person took turns in the circle. This went on for almost a half an hour. When that activity died out, a small loaf of bread was passed around from person to person on a little wooden cutting board. Each person ripped off a small chunk and put it in their mouths when it was their turn. As we did this Jeff stated that this was done in memory of Christ's body that had been broken for us. Then he showed us a cup of grape juice that he said represented a remembrance of Christ's blood that was shed for us. This cup too was passed around the circle. Many who chose to drink from this cup wiped the rim before they sipped it. I was more inspired to pass on this. My faith was not that great yet to take on other people's germs.

I felt very uncomfortable. I had no idea what to expect at this event. I was a bit anxious as I watched each activity unfold. I did not know what would happen next, my role or what was expected of me. I still felt like an outsider looking in at this very strange gathering. Plus I had arrived at four o'clock in the afternoon and now it was going on to 6pm and there was no sign of this ending any time soon. As a student with a crushing workload, this was an oppressively large amount of study time to give up. My insecurity was compounded by the feeling that there was an unwritten agenda here that was known to everyone but myself.

As the evening went on however, I started to see a pattern developing in the way the events were unfolding so I ventured to move from observer to participant. I decided to take a turn and read a verse in the *Bible* I thought was appropriate. In response I heard others say amen in support of what I had read. I then went on to explain the significance of what I read and how it applied to my own experience. What followed was not the amens and approval of the heartfelt vulnerability that I offered. I expected murmurs of understanding and agreement but instead, I was met with a cold, hard, long silence. I thought "Dear God what have I done to offend these people?" I could cut the tension with a knife so I recoiled back to my proper place, whatever that was supposed to be.

I believed I had been scolded for my boldness like a little child but I did not know why. I continued going to this event however because I was thirsty to learn more. This was a place where I could access information from new sources other than those in my own little circle of friends in the Bible Study and the Teachings on Sunday mornings. What I was learning gave me more confidence in how to live a good life which is what I thought this Christian life was all about. However each time my confidence grew, I would feel chastised for getting it wrong somehow and I would be thrown into confusion and slide back into self-doubt. The church members would try to comfort me and my obvious disappointment at said failures by kindly remind me I was still just a "Baby in Christ" and in time I would grow.

I soon decided the best action was to keep my mouth shut and just watch, listen, observe and learn. Plus even though I was learning, that did not mean I was not discerning. I had a lot of reservations about some of the ways the *Bible* was interpreted to everyday lifestyle. Sometimes what was being taught did not always seem quite right to me. However I was not concerned because I had the opinion that if someone else wanted to live a restricted life full of rules, that was OK. This would not affect me and I would choose for myself, how I would live my life and how I would interpret what I knew. In the meantime, I would keep quiet and not argue with these hard-core Christians.

What I did do however, was question Kari and Beth in private. I had many questions about the things I had seen within this church. For example, I asked about why the women wore scarves on their heads at the Breaking of Bread.

"That is a little difficult to explain", confessed Kari. "In *Corinthians* chapter eleven, a woman's hair is described as her crown and glory and it is covered as a symbol and act of humility."

"I certainly don't consider my hair as anything close to glorious", I replied, trying to lighten the discussion which had by my very questioning the church rules, had become far too serious in tone.

"This is a difficult piece of scripture to interpret", said Beth, "and I think it is best if you read this, pray about it and follow your conscience. There are a lot of things in scripture that we don't necessarily understand but God put these things in the *Bible* for a reason, for us to follow and he wants us to be obedient to Him. I think it is better to trust God's word and do what He asks.".

"I think of it as showing God that I trust Him and that I am willing to humble myself for Him. When I don't wear my head covering, I feel like I am being obstinate and proud", said Kari.

It was many months later, as I continued to question these women about the church, its habits, rules and beliefs, that I finally understood what happened to me at that very first Breaking of Bread. The feeling of tension in the room was real after all and I had been chastised by the silence. I had not imagined that or overreacted. According to scripture, women were not allowed to teach scripture in the presence of men. I could read it but not expound upon it. I had indeed broken one of the church rules at that first event. Although I had noticed it was OK to read and share like that, I had failed to notice that this was only being performed by men. According to 1 *Timothy* chapter two, "a woman must receive instruction, in submission and not exercise authority over a man".

I struggled with the UBS understanding and belief of the role of women in the home and in the church. In marriage it was the woman's duty to stay home, manage the household and raise the children. She must set a good Christian example for her family and others and teach her children about God. I was OK with that. But they also believed that a good wife would take on most of the home life work as necessary to enable her husband to be involved in the church, preach and minister without hindrances from family problems. It was giving men this free pass that I felt was a bit over-the-top. A woman staying at home was OK by me but only if it was her choice to do so.

I reconciled these extremely conservative, traditional ideas with the conviction that these rules do not apply to me. I was pursuing my career and was not planning to marry or settle down any time soon. I doubted very much that I would ever marry and if I did it would have to be to a liberal minded individual who believed in equity. I was already noticing sexist attitudes from the male professors in the university that I was already feeling a bit of angst about. I took my studies seriously and for the first time in my life as a good student, I met professors that dismissed me and my talents because I was a woman. I felt that these strange restrictive behaviours with this church were just none of my concern and if that is what they wanted to do, that was their choice.

I continued to go to the UBS events because I was accumulating a lot of *Bible* knowledge very quickly. Every time I learned something new, I soon realized that there was still so much more I did not know. My awakening experience had a huge impact on the direction of my life and decades later I can say that it still does to this present moment. I had never met people who knew the *Bible* as well as these folks. This was not just the leaders but every member from young to old. Most, if not all, could quote many verses by memory and also locate any verse you were looking for in those pages. I wanted the knowledge they had and although I spent a fair amount of time reading and studying on my own. I found I could pick up so much more by being around them and listening to their conversations. No matter what question was asked, they had an answer that could be backed up by scripture.

Although I was drawn to this group, I still remained cautious of them. As much as I liked Kari and Beth, I still did not want to open myself up to them. This was very unusual for me to do this with people. It was not like me to be so closed when making new friends. As much as I wanted to be around my new Christian friends, there was a tension there that was even more pronounced with the UBS crowd. They on the other hand were warm, welcoming, hugging types, full of laughter and wanting to have fun. Kari and Beth were always laughing uncontrollably. Kari had a smaller shy quiet laugh that presented itself in a huge smile. Beth on the other hand was loud and animated, throwing back her head of wild curls and bending over to grab her stomach. Despite everything, I could not relax, not even for a moment.

I could not understand what was wrong with me. I could not seem to get out of my own head space and just enjoy the present moment. I was constantly pushing them back to an arm's length. I imagined them being a huge vacuum cleaner trying to suck me into something that I was not yet sure about. I wanted to learn from them but not be one of them. Their lives were very regulated by their beliefs and anyone who associated with them, were made to feel like they too should live like they do. There was a lot going on between the information, overt friendliness and less tacit unseen pressures. I found myself sometimes soaking up something indiscriminately that I had to go away, think about and unpack mentally. The emotional and relationship signs and signals were not always something I could name, just feel. My circle of friends in my Bible Study and some others I had met through them, who were not members of UBS, provided a protective buffer to keep me balanced.

When I first met the people from UBS, I recalled doing a lot of reading about cults. In fact I had amassed a small collection of books on the subject. My reading taught me that a religious cult always had one charismatic leader who took on the characteristics of God, a prophet or spoke for God. The members of such groups allowed this leader to make decisions for them and they were highly secretive and segregated into a society that did not allow members to have too much contact from the outside world. The cults used a system of rewards and punishments as well as obvious physical barriers to keep outsiders from coming in and vice versa.

I looked for the similarities between the groups I read about and UBS. As far as I could see, there was not one leader and many of the members possessed similar skills as the Elders. They were very open about letting people from the outside participate. They had the backing of the university as an oversight organization. Everyone seemed to have the ability to choose to attend whatever events they wanted or not. They appeared to be a very transparent organization and were always ready to answer any questions I asked. However, I was still not convinced they were not a cult. For the life of me I could not understand why I felt this way. Plus I could not find any rational explanation for my doubts.

CHAPTER FIVE

That winter semester, I approached two of the Elders after a Sunday Teaching and asked them point blank, "Is UBS a cult?" It was as if they had not heard me. They stared at me with blank faces and just ignored the question until I walked away. Later, I put the same question to Kari and Beth in the same challenging tone. Again, I got the same response and did not even get as much as a change in expression. Why did they not answer that question? Why didn't they try to allay my fears in some way? Was my question so bizarre that they did not know how to respond? This haunted me for a long time. Maybe I was just uncomfortable because I was still considered less knowledgeable, a newbie. Perhaps this is what had been creating my sense of uneasiness. My confidence was constantly being challenged and judged, which caused me to feel embarrassed on occasion.

Correction was often given in the form of a little note under my door with a scripture verse that related to some area of my life that needed admonishment. On other occasions, Kari and Beth would drop by my dorm room with some new reading material. The information is always related to something I had said or done just prior to that as an explanation, as to why I should not have done or said what I did. The chastening was very passive aggressive. If I confronted these women or anyone else in the church about this correction, they always denied that is what they were doing. Nobody was upfront about the activities they were using to manipulate me.

Even with the new reading material and scripture quotes, I did not always agree and would find myself arguing with them in my head. However I still did not have enough evidence, proof or be able to back up what I felt was right. I still did not have enough knowledge to explain my position. Then, even if I had won the argument in my head and logically determined my actions were good, these exercises made me feel guilty nonetheless. They knew so much more than I, about how we were expected to live our lives. What if they were right and I was just being pigheaded? They were causing me to doubt myself.

The moral foundation for how I lived my life was being challenged. Kari and Beth repeatedly told me that it was the Holy Spirit that had led them to share certain information with me. Was I just being overly sensitive to criticism? Was I only imagining that the UBS members were intentionally putting pressure on me to behave and think like them? For example the Elders were teaching about the sins of fornication one Sunday morning. Then they read scripture of a whole long list of behaviours that constituted sins and would bar the doers from entering the Kingdom of God. I did not know anyone who had not sinned in these ways. I had always been fairly liberal minded and did not see sex between two people who cared for one another, or someone who was envious, ate too much or gossiped behind someone's back, were actions that warranted instant condemnation to hell. Really? There needs to be more to this. However the *Bible* verse quoted was clear. Maybe these people were right and I needed to rethink my attitude and opinions about a lot of things.

At some point into the spring semester, I sensed Kari and Beth did not approve of me going to pubs and bars. I loved to dance and meet new people. It was great fun. It seemed far from coincidental that every time I planned to go out and meet up with Tom and some of his friends at the bar, Kari and Beth would show up at my door and waylay me. Sometimes I was so late I just cancelled. I also noticed that I never saw my Christian friends at any of the drinking establishments. I asked Kari and Beth one day, "Why don't Christians go to bars and drink alcohol?"

Beth grinned at me and said, "I don't know about you but I don't enjoy drinking. I would rather spend time reading God's Word, praying or spending time in fellowship with other Christians any day?"

I responded by saying, "I don't see anything wrong with having a few drinks and laughs with friends. I enjoy it."

Kari added, "Drinking and going to bars is not setting a good Christian example for others. We must be good witnesses for Christ, especially for those who are younger in the Lord (those who have not been a Christian for long). What if someone less experienced saw you in the pub having a beer. They might think that behaviour is OK but they might not have the willpower to stop at just a couple of beers. How would you feel if that person who emulated you ended up becoming an alcoholic and ruining their lives?"

Anyway said Beth, "According to *Corinthians* we are not supposed to be bound together with unbelievers and darkness. We are supposed to be the light. We should be spending our time wisely and efficiently for the furtherance of the Gospel, not wasting it in a bar."

Clearly these UBS members were very strict and on a

path that was extremely straight and narrow. The core members and regulars attended the church's activities four out of seven days a week. I still was only prepared to go to the now three events but felt a constant pressure to do more and be more involved. In a very gentile but clear way, Kari and Beth had been trying to convince me that these activities were important for a truly devoted Christian life. With the accompaniment of scripture, they had maintained that unless you committed yourself to these things, you weren't really loving Christ. The non-devoted person was still part of the world and filled with worldly desires where the world equals bad. The UBS church even went as far as to give the impression that the attainment of a university degree was foolishness in light of the more important work God had called us to do.

Frankly I wanted my worldly desires and that is why I had paid a lot of money to finish my four year Honours degree. I loved studying, research and despite the time spent on my religious activities, was still keeping my grades up. I had even excelled in some areas and one professor was showing off my work on the Transmission Electron Microscope to others in his department. I was looking at doing some post graduate work. On the other hand my world had been shaken to the core by my conversion experience that had nothing to do with the UBS church or these women. That experience stood alone as mine to accept and work through and I could not help thirsting for more. I suppose it would be similar to someone who had experienced a UFO sighting or contact and were left compelled to study the subject for their remaining years to add meaning, proof and context to their experience.

I was not convinced by the UBS position on lifestyle, goals and they had the correct attitude. I continued to struggle with their thinking. I did not want to give up my career, my family, friends or my entire life for that matter.

I found a more balanced approach from the many other Christian friends I was now meeting through Heidi that came from a variety of different denominations. However these friends always came under criticism from Kari and Beth. They would often kindly mention how what these churches were doing was good but not great. The UBS plan was best if you compared what they were doing to what the saints in the *Bible* were doing, UBS had got it right. I had to agree with them that the followers of Jesus were fanatical and many of them lost their lives for preaching and converting people to Christianity. UBS contended that this is what God expected and this was the right and only way.

My other Christian friends largely belonged to a multi denominational group called the Navigators. This is where I started to really see and tap into the underground Christian railway of connections. Kari and Beth had placed a critical eye towards these friends and I did start to notice that none of these Christians knew half as much scripture as the UBS crowd. I enjoyed these new friends and maintained contact with them despite the feelings that perhaps UBS was right after all. They were so well versed on the *Bible* and so devoted in comparison. I started to feel a split in my thinking and an uneasiness between what I felt about UBS and what my logic and mind was telling me.

I had met so many interesting people in this Navigators group. I had also met more of Ann and Kathy's friends. I went on a pilgrimage to a Catholic monastery with a group from campus where we met up with other universities. I visited the Jesuit college and had long discussions with a Jesuit priest. I had friends that spoke in tongues and were Pentecostal. Many of the new friends were from varying kinds of Baptist churches that became confusing. I had a classmate that was Mennonite who looked like a model while another I met at a Christian conference was from a

53

very recluse order where she only dressed in black. We would talk on the phone and write to each other. She admitted she had never had a friend outside her own church. I even dated a really nice man who was pursuing the priesthood. After a few months I ended that because I did not see a future for us. What was he thinking? Decades later I saw him at a Catholic gathering of priests on TV.

Despite my uneasiness about UBS, I also saw a group of well meaning and sincere, committed folks who just wanted to proclaim their love for God. Certainly this could not be wrong or bad. I couldn't just walk away from from some dear friends who had invested so much in our friendship, been kind and caring, just because they were too devoted to God. Furthermore, other than the monks, nuns, priests and ministers I had met, I had never witnessed such faith and passion in the mainstream churches. They must be doing something right. Anyway, wasn't this exactly what God wants us to be, wholly devoted to Him and the things He wants us to do. UBS was radical and fanatical. The saints in the *New Testament* and the principles in scripture were also radical for their time and still are.

Unless you really knew the members of UBS, you would never notice anything unusual about them. However the entire lives of these people, whether they were carpenters, lab technicians or nurses, was centred around the work of their church. That work was to spread the Gospel message by word and example. Nothing else mattered as much as this one thing. Every spare moment of these people's lives was spent reading, memorizing or sharing scripture and its messages. Their homes were sparse and poorly furnished, their clothes ordinary and except for a few, their vehicles were all second hand and old. They had little or no interest in material possessions. They were all extremely committed to their cause, to their Elders and did not entertain or put up with any form of hypocrisy. When they said they didn't smoke, drink, have promiscuous sex or consume themselves with hobbies like gambling, from what I could judge, they were telling the truth.

UBS was united in purpose, ideals, theology, scriptural interpretation and its application as to how they should live their lives. They worked hard at this uniformity and for them, it seemed to be a source of focus and priority that they worked hard to achieve. That sameness gave them the strength and courage in numbers to do their work and it strengthened their faith in God and themselves. It is hard for you to doubt your beliefs when everyone you know agrees and reinforces the same vision. I guess that is why my constant questioning was a source of irritation. They could not have any ripples in the consistency and flow of thought and emotion.

UBS called themselves a *New Testament* church, wholly based on the principles, as they were written in scripture. They also patterned the structure of the church from those described in the Gospels. They believed and taught that mainstream churches of today had fallen away from the straight and narrow path by accepting liberal theology. These churches had all missed the mark of what God had intended. They said this was the reason why church attendance had been dropping for a long time. People had become disillusioned with the traditional churches and Christianity. UBS taught that they were a church not founded on the compounding errors of past churches.

UBS said it was the new wine poured into new wine skins, not old. They had the vision that it was their church, built on God's plan, that was destined to reach the entire world with the good news of the Gospel, in this generation. They took pride in being a united body of zealous, radical Christians. Only those who were chosen and who were worthy and who were one hundred percent devoted to Christ, could be accepted as a core member of this church. Anyone who left them or criticized them, were simply individuals who for any number of reasons, were not up to par and not good enough to do the work required. These people who did not unite with them, were the ones who were flawed and weak.

These concepts were not openly expressed. These were the attitudes that I detected in the whispered private conversations I overheard over many months of meetings. It was a long time of being in association with them before I understood their thinking and rationale. I was also becoming a regular attendee whom they trusted. The reason their homes were sparsely decorated and they owned few belongings was because as a *New Testament* church, they looked at their homes and belongings as temporary. They rented and did not own. They had a secret plan and I eventually had been let in on who they were and what they were trying to accomplish.

Their fervour for evangelizing, training and teaching was to build up the numbers of the membership so a new team could be sent out to form another branch of the church in another city. They were raising new Elders to take over this existing work in this town, so the more mature members could move on. The plan was to seed the country with new churches moving east and west of this one. Once the churches had spread coast to coast they would move to Europe and even Japan. The international student members of UBS were an integral part of this vision. UBS was originally an outreach church from the head of the group of international churches in the United States. They had already inundated campuses there from coast to coast, owned radio stations and had a large reserve of financial resources.

The Elders never told anyone, never mentioned it in any

literature and the university did not know who they were affiliated with. The Elders in their Teachings instead focused on growing the membership. They regularly held seminars on campus called *God's Will for Your Life*. Here the three Elders took turns outlining the churches goals to spread the Gospel and outlined the scriptural basis for how they were going to do that. They used *Bible* verses to show how it was every believer's duty to be called to preach the good news to the entire world, not just the job of a few. We were all called to be preachers and ministers. They would show how UBS was patterned after the Biblical Christian churches and that is how God had expected churches to be structured. These lectures were very simplistic and hard to refute given all the scriptural evidence provided. In short, it was God's will that everyone do what the UBS church members were doing and if your weren't with them, you were not doing God's will.

The UBS church was an evangelical and fundamentalist church meaning that it adhered to the word for word interpretation of scripture. The *Bible* was a book of laws that dictated lifestyle and how they lived their lives. I had never met a group like this in all the years of growing up and attending church. The evangelical part of that life meant they must spread the word and recruit new members. At least once a week, members would pair up and go to some of the busier areas of the city for what they called cold-turkey evangelism. Here they would approach total strangers and talk to them about Christ and who He was. The intention was to lead people into accepting Jesus as their Lord and Saviour or at least challenge them to think about it. The members used the scripture they had memorized to capture the Gospel in a nutshell in a version much like *The Five Spiritual Absolutes* pamphlet I had been given almost six months ago.

I was not interested in this proselytizing. It felt forced, dishonest and that I would be crossing a boundary to respect the privacy and space of others. People should have the freedom to be and go wherever they want without being accosted by others forcing their beliefs and opinions on them. People do not like this and I was well aware of how nasty they could get if they were being pressured into talking about something that they felt was private and none of anyone else's business. I myself would be quite rude to others who would just show up at my home to preach and share their brand of religion. No, this was not for me. I had however, started to talk about my faith with those I trusted during the natural course of sharing, as friends do.

Plus, I was very busy and did not have time for yet another church event. I continued to listen to their arguments, weathered their pressure tactics and had still not made any final conclusions as to my feelings about this church and their ideas. I was spending more and more time with Kari and Beth whom I really liked and enjoyed their company but I had taken a wait and see approach to their church. I was still learning a new language and way of looking at life. I remained focused on my split life as a devoted student dabbling in religion. When I wasn't studying, I was cross country skiing. I had a full schedule of courses during the day which only left the evenings for homework, reading and projects. I became an expert at time management. My Christian activities were carefully slotted into my work schedule.

When the spring semester ended, I was very pleased at what I had accomplished. My grades were pretty good and were in the A's and high B+s. I was not aiming for top marks anymore, just good marks. To go that extra mile and come out at the top would have taken ten times as much effort. I had promised myself that I would not just study all the time and my grades were still good enough to keep my options open to choose any career I wanted. The summer break was upon me and I had a number of decisions to make. I needed to decide where I would go for the summer to work and where I would live come the fall semester. This crossroads in my life was met with added pressure from Kari and Beth whom I was now very fond of.

"It would be great if you could stay here with us for the summer. We are going on an outreach trip up north and I know you would love it up there. It would also be a great chance for you to grow and learn more about your faith", said Beth.

"What is it like when you go on an outreach, where do you stay?", I asked.

"We split up into groups and each team spends a day or so in one town. We sleep in church halls or gyms, wherever we can find a place. Of course we take our sleeping gear with us. We eat a lot of baloney or peanut butter sandwiches. Everyone takes turns making the meals for others", explained Beth.

"That is where we first met James and Terry", piped Kari. "They came back with us and moved to the university area to join us, after we met them up north two summers ago. It was a riot because we met so many neat people. It was also a real test of faith being with the brothers and sisters all day and night for so long. We got to know each other really well and that is where some of the strongest friendships have developed", she added.

"It sounds like fun. I would really like to go with you guys this summer but I just can't decide if I should stay or go home", I explained.

Diary March 11, 1981: I can't decide what to do. Should I work near the university for the summer or go back home? I pray that God will show me which road to take. He knows the best choice for me. On Tuesday I need to make my final decision about a job offer I have at the university, without knowing if the job promised me back home is still available.

...8:00 am Tuesday morning I got a phone call from the head office of the research facility back home confirming the position I was promised was available after all. They needed an answer immediately so I said yes. I know the Lord wants me to take that job back home because He had them call me in the nick of time, just hours before I would have been forced to decide on the other job. I knew this was the right decision and it was His will. I would not be going on the outreach with Kari and Beth that summer. I feel at peace about this decision in my heart and know I am making the right choice.

I was thrilled about going home and having the opportunity to work at the world class research facility. I felt privileged to be a part of the work at his institution. Someone had pulled a lot of strings to get me here. My hard work and skills had not gone unnoticed and I had a few professors that had bragged me up to people who were in a position of influence. The decision was made and I had plans and dates to travel home. It would be a long drive and I had finally found a co-driver to travel with. Now I just needed to break the news to Kari and Beth.

Although disappointed, the main concern of Kari and Beth was for me to not stray from my faith. They were worried that without proper Christian guidance, I would lose my faith. According to UBS my family would be classified as unbelievers and I would be entering an environment that was hostile to God. They felt this anti-God influence would tear me down. They felt that it was not good for Christians, especially those who were young in their faith, to spend too much time among the heathen. This not only included our families but old friends, coworkers and virtually everyone and anyone from our past, outside the church, who had not seen the light as we had.

Kari and Beth carefully instructed me to seek fellowship with good, true Christians and to spend a lot of time reading the Word of God (the *Bible*). They told me I needed to set aside regular devotional time in prayer to maintain my faith. They gave me the name of a church to look up when I got home. This church came highly recommended to them by friends of friends. This was a Brethren church, known to be a Bible-believing organization with sound teaching. As a result of these concerns from Kari and Beth, I found myself becoming suspicious and judgmental towards others. I was told the devil himself was looking for an opportunity to devour me.

CHAPTER SIX

The summer of 1981 turned out to be quite different from the previous summer. The places were the same but the batch of this year's students were new and I was not the same person I used to be. These students were not only bright but dedicated and a lot of fun. They regularly met up with one another after work in the university lounge at the other end of the campus from where we all worked. At least twice a week they would go drinking and dancing. Two of the guys were budding comedians who would make spectacles of themselves, just for the pure joy of making everyone else laugh until they cried. I loved to dance. Dancing was the thing I was good at but every time I was invited to go with them, I refused.

I had taken Kari and Beth's suggestion to meet up with the members of the Brethren church, close to my parents home. I had already grown accustomed to the more straight and narrow lifestyle with the UBS crowd and I had stopped the frequenting pubs and bars. Most of my friends over the past semester were Christians with similar beliefs in lifestyle. My career commitments were very demanding and between the two pastimes, having fun and partying was not a priority. Now, I did not feel right about going out on the town. With all the warnings about the possibility of bad things happening to us Christians and our faith, I was apprehensive about changing my recently acquired habits. I was not sure what exactly those foretold bad things might be. One thing I was sure of was however, I had changed, become stodgy and was not much fun to be around anymore.

During the work week I stayed at my parents' place in the city near the research facility. On weekends I was at our second home, our cottage on a lake several kilometres outside an ocean community. The property was located a short driveway away from the juncture of an old highway that snakes along the scenic granite rock coastline. On Sunday mornings however, I started meeting new people at the Brethren church in town. Although I was living in close proximity to my mom and dad, I felt more distant from them than I had ever felt in my life.

Luke 9:49-50 (NAS): *And John answered and said, "Master, we saw someone casting out demons in Your name and we tried to hinder him because he does not follow along with us". But Jesus answered him, "Do not hinder him, for he who is not against you is for you."*

UBS taught us that this verse can be extrapolated on the flip side, to mean that whoever is not for you, is also not for Christ, for Christianity, for the church or for God. Therefore if a UBS member was rejected by someone when sharing the Gospel, then that person had also rejected Christ and was an enemy of God. I had tried to share my new found beliefs with my parents and other family members. I tried to point out the importance of being saved from their sins by accepting Christ. They did not want to hear what I had to say and I was devastated that I could not talk about the things that had become the focus of my life.

I loved them but a wall had been placed between us in

my mind. They were the enemy now and they were against God because they had rejected my messages. My parents were worried about the long periods of time I spent in my room every day, reading the *Bible* and praying. They saw I had changed and they could not understand what had happened to me. They did not want to hear me talk about religious stuff so I could not tell them. Even if I was able to talk about my faith, I knew they would not understand. Who would believe my story of my conversion? It is a bit of a fantastical tale really. Of course they loved me. At that time however I could not see that their love was God's love for me and that they were not the enemy at all.

I could also not explain to my parents why I was not attending the church I grew up in. My decision to switch churches baffled them. I met Brenda at the Brethren church recommended to me by Kari and Beth. What was really strange was that after meeting Brenda at church. Firstly, I had incorrectly assumed that these church folks would not be academics. Secondly, I discovered that I worked at the same research facility, on the same floor, in the laboratory adjacent to mine. This was not a small city and in the four floored building, what were the chances of that?

I was also surprised that the people at this church were extremely conservative. The congregation was very small and consisted of only fifty regulars. Men and women attended separate prayer meetings and women could not ask questions at the Bible Study. They had to present their questions to their husbands who would speak to the minister, on their behalf after the meeting was over. One man believed that any *Bible* other than the Kings James version was of the devil. The younger people had discussed how they could not go to movie theatres to watch a film. This group was a whole new layer of conservative. I could not imagine an educated woman putting up with such strict sexist rules. I was interested to see how Brenda was balancing her work as a research

65

associate and her church life.

The Sunday services were similar to those held by UBS with a little extra helping of animated fist pounding sprinkled with fire and brimstone. The songs were old traditional hymns sung in most Protestant churches with a slower tempo. There were fewer voices to cover up those voices that were off rhythm and out of tune. One fellow was deaf and belted out the songs as loud as he could. If you stood anywhere near him, you would be rendered incapable of singing along with the crowd because you couldn't hear the others.

Even though I had become ingrained in the conservative Christian circuit, I found this church just a bit too much. Too conservative, too preachy and too old style. I found the sermons overwhelmingly teetering on obnoxious. This was saying a lot for someone like me who was trying to join them to learn, watch and observe with an open mind. I stayed because of the recommendation and because for the most part, the sermons agreed with the UBS Teachings. I was at a disadvantage in being able to effectively engage with this crowd. They had their own specialized lingo and almost exclusively quoted the *King James Bible*. Their quotes were full of thees and thous. Plus they focused more on the *Old Testament* which was new territory for me.

The young people between the ages of twenty to thirty-five, met at the home of a member on Friday nights. This was for fun and fellowship, as they called it. Their brand of Christianity was ultra strict but as I got to know more of these young people, hear their stories of conversion and more about their lives, I became more comfortable. Many of these folks had not grown up in this lifestyle but had come to it later in life through conversation experiences similar to mine. As a group they had been involved in all forms of worldly pursuits before coming to this church. I had misjudged some of these folks on initial inspection and in the end, I had found a few folks who I could relate to. They were interesting people and I enjoyed getting to know them. Soon I found myself spending more social time with them and less time sequestered at home just reading, much to my parents' relief.

Brenda on the other hand was an outlier. She was raised in a strict religious Catholic family. She was the most rigid person I had ever met and she hated Roman Catholicism. She was still a strict religious person but had just changed her brand of Christianity. Having her working close by and being part of my inner core of religious friends was really difficult. It was impossible for me to keep the two worlds segregated. Brenda was not a student but a permanent lab assistant. I, on the other hand, had only been working there for two summers and associated with the students more. I really liked each one of my fellow students. We had started to bond as I laughed and carried on with them at break time.

These students were smart and most of them were headed to medical school in the fall. Only those with the highest grades could work there. They continued to pressure me to party with them. This stirred up a furious conflict in me because I could not understand why I was not supposed to go. I wanted to go but had been told repeatedly that true Christians don't go to parties. I needed a better explanation than that. I told Brenda that I had planned to stop by the student union pub that evening, to meet up with the other students.

What a fiasco. According to Brenda that was just the worst plan ever. Brenda told me I was supposed to be in the world, not of the world. I would be a terrible Christian witness and example, if I went someplace where I knew there would be dancing, drinking and alcohol. She said this event would lead me into sin and I belonged to Christ. She said I should not even be associating with sinners in the first place. On top to that she said I would ruin the reputation of her church and all my new friends who attended that church. She even admitted to me that she did not play cards, drink alcohol, watch TV, go to movies or wear any clothing that showed skin above the elbows or knees. Boy was she uptight.

In my heart I could not really believe this was true. Brenda made it sound like a one way ticket to hell for just a few hours of fun. What was wrong with having a bit of fun? Brenda's adamant rationalization and conviction caused me to doubt my own sensibilities, especially when what she said was the same as what Kari and Beth told me. I tried to mentally align this explanation with scripture I had read and what I felt was right. The best evidence I could come up with to support my gut feeling was that Jesus loved everyone, including sinners and spent most of his time with them.

I challenged Brenda with my new rationale but she would not budge on her premise. She started quoting all kinds of other verses from the *Bible*. She had an entire arsenal of ammunition I did not have and she was quick on the draw. She was ready for me. I made a few brief phone calls to other church people and they all had the same beliefs that Brenda had. I could not win and did not really want to win. I just wanted to reconcile my instincts, gut feel and heart knowing with what they were telling me. The subject remained unresolved for me and that week, I refused all my invitations to party. I was a new Christian, what did I know?

Towards the middle of the summer I had become more comfortable with both sets of friends, co-workers and the church gang. There were four of us student researchers that became particularly close. There was Lara, Jerry, Scott and myself. During breaks at work, we always hung out, talked and joked around. Jerry was one of the funny ones while Lara and I just clicked. All four of us spent a lot of time discussing our plans and dreams. These relationships started to gel as we approached mid summer. I started to loosen up a bit and tried and regained some of my common sense approach to lifestyle. I eventually decided to let the conundrum go and enjoy myself at one of these weekly parties. These were my friends after all.

At the end of the first party at Lara's house, I was asked why I waited so long to come. I was totally honest with them about what I had been going through, about my Christian faith and conversion. Scott, Lara and Jerry were genuinely interested in my story and they too opened up about their own beliefs. That is when Lara showed me her altar and that is when the four of us became closer. Lara and I both had a strong religious faith but we came to this from different directions. She was Indian, Hindu and had a little altar in her flat. We became so close that by the end of the summer she gave me a silver friendship ring that matched hers.

I had become more confident in my position that going to parties was OK as a Christian and continued to go to the weekly parties. Then to celebrate the end of summer, a weekend canoe trip was planned for us. I had a car and the group needed another driver. I happened to bump into Brenda in the hall just after the trip was announced. I had been on this particular trail and portage route before, loved the area and told her I was going. She strongly disapproved of my decision. Her reaction was over the top and I was aggravated by her reaction. I wasn't asking for her permission or advice. I was also annoyed at being made to feel guilty about associating with some really great people. So what if they weren't born-again converts to Christianity.

I told Brenda that Jesus would not have avoided these people because they weren't "saved". He would have loved them and spent time with them just as described in the *New Testament*. I told her that I really cared about these people who were not just people, they were my friends and it is kindness and love that counts. I said this to her in an authoritative voice. I was angry with her and had enough of this game of guilt and rules. Brenda was taken aback by my response to her indignation with me. Later on she sent me a card with a note in it saying that even though I was a baby in Christ, she could still learn from me. She added that I had really challenged her and caused her to do some thinking. This was her olive branch apology to reach out to me while maintaining the integrity of her self proclaimed superiority. I was starting to get weary of this hierarchy of status within this true loving Christianity I was learning about.

Someone convinced Brenda to come to one of the last parties of the summer season. It may have been my discussion with her, I was not sure. She herself had been under pressure by her colleagues to participate more with the students. I wasn't drinking and had not used alcohol much since my conversion experience. This was not a Christian thing but because I did not like feeling tipsy and getting hangovers. I was having a great time dancing up a storm with everyone else when I first saw Brenda standing alone, next to a table. She was the only person not dancing.

A while later I caught her eye and noticed a look of disgust, with a virtual dagger purposely delivered in my direction. She was sending me a clear signal to stop me from doing something. I then remembered that in her world, Christians were not supposed to dance. I was disappointed that the self doubt I had been struggling with all summer, washed over me again like a tidal wave. I continued dancing but it lost the fun factor. Were my body movements too seductive, sinful? What was it? Was I causing someone else to sin?

By now the summer was coming to a close. I had met some really great people, made new friends and narrowed the gap of separation between state and church in my life. I managed to attend church and enjoy a small circle of Christian friends with a more common sense approach to their faith. Brenda never said anything negative about her fellow church goers but I know by some of her comments, she considered them as lesser Christians. At the same time I managed to socialize with my newfound research, non-Christian friends.

In the beginning I was almost afraid to interact with non-believers. I was warned by multiple people that I would lose my faith and become "tainted by the world" as they put it. I did not "backslide" or "revert to old ways" as was predicted. Instead I enjoyed myself with some really wonderful people from both ends of the religious to non-religious spectrum, who all taught me more about my faith. However I still had an underlying perception that non-believers were different. They continued to exist on the other side of a barrier wall. This division between us and them remained.

CHAPTER SEVEN

Something had significantly shifted over the spring semester and summer break. I noticed a difference when I returned to my university program for that third fall semester, far from home. Whatever it was, I can look back and see that my personality was not the same. I had changed. I distinctly remember feeling weak from fighting my inner doubts about all the doctrine and dogma I had been learning. It was a lot to sort through and I remember asking myself for the millionth time, if this UBS church was a cult. I was worn out from fighting and questioning yet another religious interpretation of scripture that did not sit well with me. I could not grasp why I persisted in my polarized reluctance to trust these Christians.

All my regular friends, not involved in UBS, were now also believers and dedicated Christians. All my new Christian friends, I had met outside of UBS, belonged to a wide variety of Christian denominations and all of them believed in the same tenets of faith. Their doctrines and scriptural interpretations were similar to the UBS crowd. The difference was in how each denomination applied those principles to daily living. UBS was not any different in philosophical thinking but what set them apart from the other groups was their fanaticism and high standards. Was that so bad?

It was at the beginning of September 1981, that I chose to stop struggling with my doubts about UBS. My mind was exhausted from challenging everything that my heart could not fathom. I decided to find a way to squelch the imbalance by accepting the UBS Teachings within reason. I would suppress my inner critic and concentrate on learning. There was still so much more knowledge I needed and I was not in a position to argue unless I had a better understanding. When questions arose inside me, or red flags were waving, as per my usual state of being, I would ruminate only momentarily, then let it go. I would no longer let myself become distracted by these hauntings. They were the experts, not me.

This simple and what seemed to me, at the time, logical choice was the most crucial decision I had made since my conversion. At that time I did not have the depth of experience in this brand of Christian faith to detect the subtle differences between fringe groups like UBS and other fundamental evangelicals like Four Square, Two By Twos, Brethren, Amish, Old Order Mennonite, various Evangelical, Reformed or Southern Baptists and the Pentecostals. These religious groups were nothing like the mainstream churches I grew up with. I attended Sunday school at the United Church and all my friends growing up who were Protestant or Roman Catholic, lived similar Christian lifestyles as our families. This letting go of the things that I didn't fully understand, accelerated my journey into a world where I ceased to exist.

All the churches I had ever experienced had similar governing structures of authority, responsibility, accountability and oversight. Individual churches were off-shoots of a larger collection with frameworks at each level for input and reporting. All had priests or ministers that worked for the congregation with the assistance of deacons or lay people. UBS was unusual in that it had three ministers. It was much later before I was entrusted with information about UBS's affiliations, reporting, accountability, power structures, long term goals and future plans.

My plan for that fall semester was that I would live with four other Christian women I had met through the Navigator's organization. We had made arrangements to rent a house right on the edge of campus. It belonged to a college professor who was away on sabbatical. The house was a four bedroom side-split on a private residential property with mature trees, lawns and gardens. It was on the same street that Jeff and the brothers lived and where the UBS Sunday night gathering met. This house was a great find and I was excited to get away from the dorm life even though I would no longer see Tom and Pam outside of class. Ann had been spending more time with her Jesuit friend and travelling to South American in her time off. Kathy was a year ahead and had already graduated and moved back home.

The Navigators is an organization that helps train leaders to work in their respective denominational churches. The Navigators, like UBS, was classified as a club on the university campus that provided activities, Bible studies and teaching material to students. Our household was one of many scattered around town and was put together by Navigator leaders. Because of the non-denominational nature of the organization, our little team of five candidates included one from each of Mennonite, Roman Catholic, Brethren, Pentecostal and UBS. The household included Julie, Amy, Angela, Lorraine and myself who were all women I met through Heidi. I was nominated because I started to become known for my own brand of zealousness.

The household was well structured with rules and expectations. Each of us had to agree to how the living arrangements would be run, before being accepted into the house. Every evening at five o'clock, one person was assigned to make supper for everyone. The remaining four washed the dishes, dried them, put them away and swept the floor. Those chores were rotated daily. The laundry, vacuuming, grocery shopping and yard work was scheduled weekly and daily. Even the meals were per-planned before the designated person did the required shopping. Everyone was well informed about what they were signing up for. Anyone who had doubts or objections were excluded as candidates. We had the whole summer to opt out and there was a waiting list of hopefuls ready to take our places.

These arrangements worked very well and the workload was light because everyone did their part. Lorraine, Julie and myself had our own rooms. Amy and Angela shared the master bedroom. I was glad to continue the privacy that I had when I was in residence and was relieved to have a quiet place to study when I needed it. Judy was the more serious student in the house, I had good grades but was not on the path to high honours like Judy was. Not only did she study all the time but she was well disciplined, well organized and punctual. She went to bed and got up at the same time every day, was well groomed, polite and even tempered. She left the rest of us in awe. Nobody challenged her when she asked for her own room.

Then there was Lorraine who was the opposite of Judy. She too had her own room but for a different reason. Lorraine was very excitable and once she started down a particular mindset or started to laugh, it was difficult for her to stop or change direction. She was loud and laughed wholeheartedly, uncontrollably and often. When the pendulum would swing the other way she could become sad or upset, crying as if on the brink of despair. Lorraine could be absent minded but most often was bubbly and talkative. Rarely was there a pause at middle ground.

Lorraine met her fiance that previous semester and all five of us were fully involved in the highs and lows of her wedding plans. She would eat bananas coated in peanut butter when stressed which I too adopted later in life. The fiancee was just over six feet tall and very slim. He had a huge appetite and when he came for a meal, Lorraine cooked and we doubled the amounts of food. Half for him and the rest for the five of us. One meal was Chili Con Carne and halfway through eating Lorraine casually mentioned that the can of beans was bulged out before opening. That initiated another drama as we immediately ended the meal and interrogated her about the can. Then we waited for days to see if any of us got sick. None of us were sure how we could handle being close to her, for extended periods of time so early on, we had unanimously agreed that Lorraine would have her own room.

Amy and Angela had been close friends since childhood, had gone to high school together and now were together in university. They were both very quiet conservative and sensible women. Amy was a Roman Catholic and was not very outspoken about her faith. Unfortunately for Amy, there was a strong anti-Catholic sentiment circulating between members of the more fundamental, evangelical protestant churches on campus. UBS was blatantly and open in expressing these same biases. The beliefs of the other denominations in this discrimination only reinforced for me, that the UBS Teaching was the correct one. It was not long before Amy became aware of my damaging attitudes. She was deeply hurt by what she discovered and could not understand why she was being singled out by myself and others.

Through the Sunday Teachings and the lectures on other religions, the Elders openly talked about their anti-

Catholic views and the problems with the Roman Catholic church. Ron often used a quote from *The Catholic Chronicles* by Keith Green that he felt accurately summed up what UBS believed. The quote was from Dr. E.C. Cole that said:

Romanism is a complicated system of salvation by works. It offers salvation on the instalment plan, then see to it that the poor sinner is always behind in his payments so that when he dies there is a large unpaid balance and he must continue payment by suffering in purgatory or until the debt is paid by prayers, alms and the sufferings of his living relatives and friends. The whole system and plan calls for merit and money from the cradle to the grave and beyond. Surely the wisdom that crew such a plan of salvation is not from God.

This basic and rather simple understanding, taught by UBS, was an accepted belief shared by a variety of protestant churches on campus. However UBS was more open and louder about this, just as they were about everything else. This fit with the UBS reputation that bordered on fanaticism. The members of UBS considered this a compliment not a criticism. They believed that Satan was alive and well and working through people as their enemy. Any persecution they received was the work of the devil through non-Christian, ungodly folks manipulated by evil forces. To be harassed when sharing your beliefs was a sign you were on the right track, gaining ground for the kingdom of God.

To be a fundamentalist, you were a person who took what was written in the *Bible* literally with a simplistic interpretation. I had been studying and comparing different religions through my fundamental beliefs and saw how most churches had strayed from the basic teaching of the *Bible*. The devil's biggest weapon was to deceive people by making a counterfeit copy of The Truth. Only those trained in spiritual matters, by studying the *Bible*, could discern the true churches from the false ones. Therefore it was important to carry your cross daily and stand up for the Word of God despite persecution. Everyone needs to hear this truth, or as UBS believed was Their Truth, in order to be saved from an eternity in hell. The enemy, Satan, was roaring like a lion, stalking about in a world full of lies, looking for someone to devour.

The doctrines of fundamentalist churches were not complicated or difficult to understand and share. The Catholic religion on the other hand was complicated, deep and encompassed thousands of years of tradition and history. It was easy to see how those with the simpler faith could easily misunderstand Catholicism. UBS called the use of icons, idol worship for example. Alms and penance was buying a place in heaven through works and not faith. Because of the inability to grasp the many layers, they translated what they observed, to fit their very simplistic view of the world.

Many prayers were said for the salvation of the Roman Catholics. UBS went further and considered the Catholic church to be a cult with incorrect doctrine along with the Mormons, Jehovah Witnesses and others. I did not come right out and tell Amy I thought she was doomed but I was clear about my unfavourable opinion of her Roman Catholic church. The misunderstandings being perpetuated were compounded by the fact that most Catholics themselves could not explain, prove, or defend their own faith when faced with such attacks. Amy was one such Catholic. When an eternity of Heaven versus Hell is questioned, keeping quiet was not an option and I felt people needed to hear my truth to wake them up. I had become one such zealous, pain-in-the-ass, evangelical Christian.

On campus, some of the professors were teaching about

the Occult while others had been ridiculing Christianity in the classrooms, as was reported to us by our UBS leaders. I was told it was my duty to have the courage to confront these professors. When one of my advanced classes was being instructed in the fine details of the Theory of Evolution, I spoke up. UBS and other churches felt that this topic in particular denied the work of our Creator and that the underlying premise was just wrong. Many Christian groups on campus had been promoting scientific facts to disprove evolution. There had been high profile public debates on the topic. Dr. Wider-Smith, a famous author and scientist came to our campus and debated on behalf of us Creationists.

My questions regarding the validity of the Evolutionary Theory, as described by my professors, created a lot of drama in my classes. I could see the way they looked at me. I was one of Those people. I became instantly unpopular and my classmates were angry with me. One professor took my questions as a personal attack when I said the theory went against God and Christianity. He became very upset and explained that he too was a Christian but that this science did not negate that. I maintained that this was just that, a theory. I told him and my classmates, "To teach this theory, as a fact, only gives people looking for a reason to not believe in God, proof for their disbelief."

My faith had been growing, or rather my confidence that my faith had been growing, was growing. My knowledge of the *Bible*, the Christian doctrines and apologetics was being honed. As a result, I was gaining courage to be more outspoken and my skin was getting more calloused as my willingness to challenge others increased. I had arrived at a point where I felt I could logically defend and prove my faith. For myself and fellow church members this was a sign of Christian maturity. The negative reactions to my preaching was just the expected rejection of non-believers, for doing the right thing. I chose to think this way. However a creeping suspicion was welling up inside of me. This persecution may not be the result of righteous actions. Rather, it was more likely to be the result of my obnoxious behaviour.

CHAPTER EIGHT

By the end of my third, fall semester I had gathered many friends from a wide range of Christian denominations. I had grown in a direction that pulled me further away from my classmates. I rarely saw them anymore. My roommates had invited me to many events at their own churches. We had a policy to include each other in all our extracurricular activities. This added a layer of richness to the camaraderie of the Navigator household. It was a great experience for all of us. This broadening of my Christian connections however, did not detach me from my friendship with Kari and Beth. They still remained my closest friends and I still preferred the UBS church. I saw it as a place of action where the members had more Biblical knowledge, were passionate about their faith and more devoted than any other group I had encountered.

During my last and fourth semester some cracks developed in the Navigator household between myself and my roommates. I started to see that the zeal I exhibited in my own brand of faith was considered too over-the-top by my roommates. I realized that they did not wholeheartedly approve of UBS but they could not explain to me why. All they could say was that it was too fanatical for their comfort level. In return I noticed I had become more critical of them and started to pick out practices that I saw as incorrect. I knew they loved their faith but I thought they were not devoted enough to appreciate the UBS church. I had decided that they were just too materialistic and caught up in the ways of the world.

Unknown to me, a couple of months prior to graduation, Kari and Beth approached the Elders about having me join their UBS household. The three Elders agreed to give their permission, only if they were convinced I was committed to the goals of UBS and the Christian lifestyle they practised. They made arrangements to meet with me for an interview. I did not know why they wanted to meet with me. I was asked to come to the UBS office in the Student Union Building at lunchtime. All three men were there with just me, which I thought was very odd. I did not know they even knew I existed and had rarely spoken to them even though I was a regular part of their community. It was not until many months later that I understood what this meeting was all about.

The discussion started out very friendly with perfunctory small talk. Then the storytelling began about the history of UBS and how it was founded. UBS originated from a collection of churches in the United States. During the Vietnam War two Christian men met during a very difficult event, in battle, on the front lines. They shared their faith with one another and discovered that they had similar ideas about Christianity. They became friends and continued that friendship after returning home. I learned that together these two soldiers and a third man, were the founding members of the group of international churches, from which UBS was born as an outreach, satellite church.

They told me that UBS was founded on the belief that Christianity needed to go back and start over using the basics of scripture to create a *New Testament* church, just like the ones founded by the Apostles. That this group of churches would be a radical movement that would do away with the generations of compounded errors that had weakened modern day churches. Their church would do God's calling, God's work, in God's way, using the framework described in the *Bible*. They believed that they could reach the entire world with the Gospel in this current generation. They called their outreach missions The Blitz. This was the mission that Jesus had given his followers a long time ago, that was never fulfilled. They believed that they would be the ones to complete that mission.

The most senior Elder, Ron, had heard one of the founders preaching at a rally in California and was inspired to follow this same dream and vision. He was originally from this university town but was trained by senior leaders in the United States. When he returned home, he recruited his friend Jeff and together they started this branch called UBS. The founders and most senior leaders were the brothers that the UBS Elders looked up to and tried to emulate. The UBS doctrine and Teachings were the same as that taught by the founders. The UBS tape library included a variety of sermons on topics from the founders such as *The Family, God's Recruiting Program, Dealing with Church Problems, Why Jesus?, Radical Christianity* and *God's Will for Your Life.*

The February 1983 issue of *The Cause* (a magazine for all the affiliated churches) quoted one of its founders as saying the following, when he was in Vietnam: "Every night I would look up into the sky through the fire of tracer bullets, I would see the heavens and realize that my life was but a fleeting shadow and to do anything but give all to Jesus, is the most absurd futility that one could possibly imagine." This history, background and philosophy and the story of these founders was a chance for the Elders to see how aligned I was with the goals of their church. This was

85

my initiation into the core membership, as part of the leadership in training, for the church.

Following this meeting Kari and Beth asked me to join their household. That is when they told me about the plan and why the Elders had met with me. I accepted the invitation. They had a three bedroom basement apartment, on an older tree lined street that was a twenty-five minute walk from campus. Like most UBS households it was sparsely furnished. I was loaned a single bed and a night table. I shared the largest bedroom with Beth and she made room in her clothes closet for my stuff. Kari had her own room as did Donna. Kari and Beth were considered the older sisters in Christ while Donna and I were the younger mentees in training.

Diary April 20, 1982: Lord, thank you for giving me such a great place to stay with such great women. I really pray that we will learn from one another. Teach me how to encourage others and increase my wisdom so I won't be so legalistic, meaning that things are only one way and that is it. I want to build up the women around me. Forgive me for boasting about my knowledge which is actually very little. I pray that you will provide a bed and some furniture. I know Lord, that you provide everything according to our needs. Thank you.

Donna had been with UBS for a few years and had graduated from a Bible College. However even though she had formal training in theology and scripture, she was considered younger in the maturity of her faith, than those that had been with UBS longer. Christian age was considered as the length of time since you had first seriously committed your life to Christ or had been born-again through a conversion experience. The length of time in the UBS church was also a factor. Fundamentalist Christians had two birth dates, one physical, the other spiritual. The spiritual age determined your placement and rank within the UBS church hierarchy. Younger brothers and sisters in their faith were expected to respect and follow the example, guidance and coaching of their Elders.

I was now working on campus as a laboratory technician in the Plant Science Department. I had given up the opportunity to work on my Masters degree with a prominent professor. I was of two minds about this but was pressed into thinking that this was a worthless worldly pursuit. Now that I was no longer a student, I had more time to devout to church activities. All of us roommates worked on campus in some capacity. We did everything together including hiking to the nearby gorge or conservation area. Sometimes we took trips into the Big City to visit art galleries or explore Chinatown. If we did not have something planned, we were at a church event. Most evenings Beth would drive us to the campus in her little baby blue Volkswagen Bug for our outreach assignments.

UBS strongly believed in evangelizing to win others to the faith. Commitment to evangelism and outreach activities were considered a sign of maturity. By doing so, it showed that you had arrived and been trained enough to become a productive functioning member of the church. A high level of zeal was expected by the membership and sharing our faith with others was part of that. Any spare time we had was supposed to be spent in sharing our faith. The Elders preached that if we were faithful sharing our beliefs and filled with the Holy Spirit, God would use us to bring about the conversion experience in others. That was the Lord's command to "go forth into the world baptizing others in the name of the Father, Son and Holy Ghost." The Disciples of Christ gave their lives to spreading this same message of the Gospel. We were expected to pattern ourselves after these Saints.

Formal evangelism was always done in pairs. In our

household Kari and Beth were a paired team. They were the experienced ones. Donna and I were their offspring, in a manner of speaking, and because we were deemed not experienced enough to go on our own, Kari and Beth split up to take on Donna and myself as partners. Donna went with Kari and I went with Beth. Because I was in training, I was instructed not to speak but to just observe and pray for Beth as she worked. Kari and Beth were responsible for the church membership for us and if we had any questions, we must first ask them. We were their charges.

Beth and I went out to the campus to talk to students at least two nights a week. Fear of evangelizing was considered a lack of maturity and that you still possessed a certain amount of pride. That was considered a bad thing, in fact sinful. Instead we had to be faithful and obedient to do the things God wanted us to do. God wanted all His children to return to Him like the prodigal son. Because the university had a summer semester, there were a lot of students on campus all year long. We most often started in the cafeteria of the Student Union Building. Beth would look for someone who was sitting alone and we would go over and introduce ourselves.

For a long time I just tagged along silently. When we had concluded our impromptu meeting with a stranger, Beth would sit down with me and review what happened. Then she started getting me to practice my spiel with her at home, making sure I hit all the important points and scripture verses outlining the steps to salvation. More and more Beth let me speak during a meeting with a stranger. Then, after each encounter, we would sit down and analyze my words, motives, feelings and reactions. My intent and the attitude of my heart, was just as important as what I said. Beth always had suggestions for how I could improve and lessons on what areas needed work as we tried to understand both ourselves, our team dynamic and each person we approached. This was serious business.

As usual we started in the cafeteria and this particular evening we spotted a woman sitting in the large eating area in the far corner of the building. The windows there overlooked the central campus, towards the library. She did not see us approach her and she never looked up as we stepped toward her table.

Beth spoke to her saying, "Hi, my name is Beth and we belong to a group on campus called University Bible School. Are you a student?"

The young woman replied, "Yes, my name is Janet."

"Now that I see what you are reading, I take it you are taking Psych 200. I took that course too. You must be in your second year of Arts, or are you taking this as an elective?", asked Beth.

"It is just an elective. I'm in Environmental Biology and this is my second year", said Janet

"Brian, who is in our church, took Environmental Biology and graduated two years ago. He is now working for Dextron. He monitors and is working on controlling the affluent that runs into the Speedway River. He really liked the courses he took while he was here. He likes working in his field even more so he can balance his time and be more involved in the church", chatted Beth.

"I hope I can get a job in the industry", said Janet with a big sigh.

Beth added, "Every week we wander around campus to talk to people about Christ. Many people have not heard, or do not understand, the basic Gospel message. Since we are with a campus church, we would like to share some information with you and discuss any questions you might have about Christianity. Do you belong to a church or religious group?"

"Yes, I was brought up in the United Church. I go to church once in a while but I find it hard to go when I have so much school work to do. I don't really like to discuss my beliefs with other people because I feel my faith is personal", said Janet uncomfortably.

"Yes, it is something very personal. I agree. I believe that our relationship with God is like a friendship. We can have a personal relationship with Christ. What we come to talk to people about is not this relationship, or what you believe as much, it is just the sharing of information. We want to make sure that people have all the facts about who Christ is and what He did for us. In that way people can have a good foundation, on which to base their beliefs. There is so much misinformation and misunderstanding surrounding the Gospel", replied Beth.

"Isn't the Gospel just the good news that Christ preached about us loving one another?", said Janet.

"Yes, that is part of it. It is also about the fact that we are all sinners and are separated from God. The good news is that Jesus died for our sins to pay the penalty so we can be reconciled to God. By accepting what Christ did on the cross to pay our debt and by accepting Christ as Our Lord, we can have that relationship with God again. We are forgiven and those who accept Christ's sacrifice will be saved from eternal damnation. We all have a choice to either admit our sins and accept God's forgiveness and accept Christ, or reject the opportunity. God stands at the door to our heart and knocks and waits for us to open that door and invite Him into our lives in a meaningful way." explained Beth.

"I have heard some of this before. But I have never

heard it put quite that way. I'm not sure I believe we are all sinners. Isn't that just a bit extreme?", replied Janet.

Beth started to say, "The *Bible* says..."

Janet interjected by saying, "...Listen, I really have to get some work done. I don't want to argue about this. I can't quote scripture to back up what I believe. I just know these things."

Beth countered her by saying, "Sometimes we can be misled. The *Bible* is the Word of God and is the source of what we believe. It is better to base our lives on that. I would encourage you to read some of the things in this little pamphlet. If you have any questions about this, please call us. I will give you a number to call".

"Thanks but I really have to get some work done", finished Janet.

We said goodbye to Janet and moved to another part of the building. I had remained silent and prayed mentally for Beth throughout the discussion. I remained engaged in the conversation instead by looking interested and nodding in agreement with Beth. As time went on I contributed more and more to these conversations. Most of the time we approached single women, women in pairs, or male/female couples. We rarely talked to more than three people at once. The goal was to find out as much as possible about that person's faith. Then we could segue into that aspect of their own beliefs. If the person refused to open up to us, we would just leave the pamphlet, read a scripture verse and then walk away and pray instead.

Most of the time we were able to get people to talk to us by being friendly and finding some common ground in their life experience that matched ours. If the person became belligerent, we did not walk away or back down.

We just remained calm, agreed with them and the outburst and then asked more questions about what they said. We would keep this up to disarm them in the hopes we could engage them in a reasonable conversation. The first part of the talk was just small talk so we could observe, question, listen and size up who this person was. From there we would evaluate the answers they gave regarding their own faith experience and beliefs. We tried to shore up any deficiencies we saw that needed added understanding. Then we would use that weak area to segue to the related aspect of the Gospel message we were trying to communicate. Then we would build the rest of the steps to salvation around that.

Many people challenged us with difficult questions. We always tried to back up our answers with scripture verses and logic. That meant we had to memorize a lot of scripture and be able to locate and reference them on the fly. Our purpose and goal was not to win every argument but to challenge them back and get them to think more about their position. Plus we always tried to sneak in as much of the Gospel message as possible, to give them some actionable things to do. Jeff was the Elder that oversaw the campus and student aspect of the church. He taught us various approaches to evangelism and how to share the Gospel. Most of our training however, came from our own personal encounters with our supervising mentors and the lessons learned by our colleagues.

In the beginning I hated these evangelism assignments. However I put this off as pride and just forced myself to go. Plus Beth and Kari could tell when Donna and I were just making excuses not to go and would give us the push and pep talk we needed. I knew it would be a good learning experience. Once I got started, I enjoyed the challenge and the rush of overcoming my fear. I did enjoy talking about my faith and the thrill of walking up to a complete stranger and sharing such an intimate truth about myself. It was a difficult subject for anyone to talk about and somewhat scary because some people did turn nasty.

For the most part I only met a few of these folks. Most people were interesting and I felt blessed to have had the opportunity to meet them. With every new encounter I learned something new about myself. The questions I could not answer motivated me to continue learning, rethink my faith and engage in more research to find answers. I was learning how to dig deep, understand who I was, what I believed, what was true in life and how to connect to others in a meaningful way. That was a valuable life skill that would benefit me for the remainder of my life.

CHAPTER NINE

The summer of 1982 was my first summer away from home in a long time. Now that I was no longer a student, there would be more time for church activities, getting to know other UBS members and doing some evangelizing. Even though I worked during the day as a Research Assistant, I hoped that this would be a time to devote to my church and my faith. I wanted to develop some habits of regular prayer and scripture reading to form a daily devotion to God as was suggested by UBS, as well as the Navigators, that we all needed to do. I was now living with Kari and Beth whom I greatly admired and respected. This town was beautiful in the summer and I was looking forward to exploring and hiking with my roommates.

The only friend I had now, that I considered to be non-religious, was Tom. We remained good friends and still kept in touch right up until graduation day. Now he had gone back home, along with Pam who I had not spoken to for many months. The friends I made through Navigators had continued on in their household to finish their studies. I had to move out because I was no longer a student. Now that I was in a UBS household, all my Christian friends were in the same church. I soon lost touch with all my friends outside of UBS.

UBS decided to organize all its members into three teams for the summer. Each household was assigned by district and we were expected to attend all the church activities within our own group. In effect UBS split the church into three smaller church groups with one Elder leading each one. Each mini-church was called a Bible Discussion Group (BDG). All events for all three BDGs were held simultaneously but at three different locations. The weekly Bible Study, the Sunday night Breaking of Bread and Prayer Meetings were all held within the assigned BDG. Only the Sunday morning Teaching and Thursday evening classes on religion were to be attended by all members together. These two events were always open to the public and we welcomed anyone who wanted to attend.

I was no longer a student and under the jurisdiction of Jeff. Now, as part of Kari and Beth's household, we were placed under the leadership of Ron. We did not waste any time getting involved in the evangelistic outreach activities we were expected to do. However, the new BDG assignments three evenings a week, my nine to five job and the two Sunday gatherings left little free time. Beth and I were using our lunch breaks and evenings before and after church gatherings, to meet with people on campus. We called this cold-turkey evangelism and it was something I needed to get up to speed on doing well. Most of the time we stuck to the campus buildings but sometimes we even went door to door in the community.

Diary May 25, 1982: Lord, thank you for the cool, clean, fragrant air and the rich green foliage. The birds sound so cheerful. I guess that is because they totally depend on You and You care for them. I pray that today I could delight in You too. Help me to forget myself and trust You to fill me with Your Spirit. Cause me to say and do good things. Help me to be myself today, to be totally free and trusting You.

Diary June 1, 1982: *At noon today we spoke with Jane. She is a Muslim from Malaysia. We didn't succeed in getting the Gospel message out to her. We also approached Kathy and Ned. She did not want to talk at first but in the end she was open and I shared the Gospel message with both of them.*

Diary June 2, 1982: *This evening we met Lila visiting from another university. She was very antagonistic at first but became more open. Beth and I shared the Gospel and our presentation was close to the Five Spiritual Absolutes pamphlet. Then we approached Jackie, a high school student. She was very open and we shared the Gospel using the pamphlet as well, with her.*

Diary June 3, 1982: *On the noon break we tried to talk to the Blonde woman from the main desk in the Student Union Building. She was very nervous and no Gospel was shared. We were however able to share the Gospel with Janet from Malaysia. She agreed with some of the points but did not agree that Jesus was the Son of God. We also saw Charles and Andy from the church.*

Diary June 7, 1982: *This evening we spoke with one woman who studied the Bible for six years. We shared the Gospel with her. Mary, who was a Roman Catholic, did not want to talk to us. We shared a verse from 2Thessalonians with her. We talked to Paula for a long time and were able to share a lot of information with her. We shared the Gospel but she does not believe Jesus is the Son of God. Virginia and Jack, also Roman Catholics, said that they want to know God and believe everything in their lives is OK, as is. We did not share the Gospel with them. Allan, he talks to God a lot and knows Him as his Lord.*

Diary June 8, 1982: Talked to Darlene at noon. She went to the same school as Donna. We shared the Gospel with her and I believe she is a Christian.

Diary June 10, 1982: Lord, thank you for allowing us to speak to all these people on evangelism assignments. Thanks for answering all our prayers as we talk to people. Thank you for helping and encouraging me through those tough times this week and for teaching me that I need to change my attitude.

Diary June 11, 1982: Lord, I need help in memorizing scripture daily and in reading through nine chapters of scripture each day. I ask You Lord to help me with this. One of my goals was to study the Word more this summer. Please make that happen by increasing my diligence.

In mid summer, I attended the World Challenge Regional Conference with my roommates and many others from UBS. This conference was for all the international groups of churches and was held at a university town in the central United States. We arrived with our sleeping gear, were divided up and then billeted to the homes of our sisters who lived near the conference. We did not get much time to relax or get to know our hosts because we had to go directly to a seminar at the largest auditorium on campus. There were so many people, some standing at the back and others sitting in the isles. The entire weekend was packed with seminars from early morning until eleven pm at night. We only had short breaks for meals that were provided in that university's cafeterias.

Two of the three founding members of the conglomerate of our international churches, spoke to thousands from Michigan, New York, Indiana, Missouri, Maryland, South Carolina, Ohio and Canada. The seminars consisted of sermons, songs, prayers and lectures on many topics. We all kept notes like good students.

Summer Conference Notes 1982: *To keep in love with Jesus, He wants our hearts and our love for God as our motivation. We give our life to Christ by giving our life to people. We are all priests if we are satisfied in Christ. We are proclaimers. We must learn from and obey God according to His Word and love others. Jesus is our example. We must serve. Seeking our own interests is sin. God wants us all to be saved.*

When we are in contact with unsaved people and they don't hear God's message, we are not in God's will. Take the example of Peter who tried to walk on water. I would rather get wet trying than to stay in the boat and stay dry. Jesus rebuked Peter. The others were not worthy of rebuke. We should get rebuked. We are ambassadors for Christ and we must bear fruit by influencing others. We must do all things for the sake of the Gospel. We must change our life because we have a radical message and must live a radical life. We must run to win.

The way to do this is to be united and intent on one purpose. We must do things that seek the good of our neighbour. If we are a friend of the world we are enemies of Christ. We can't serve two masters because one will suffer. If we are lukewarm, God will spit us out. Whatever you do, do for the glory of God. What we believe is what we receive and faith is the key. This is not the hour of peace. We are at war. Jesus came to bring division and fire. Our goal is not to save everyone but to tell everyone.

We need spiritual, experiential prayer and financial support before moving forward. There must be a systematic plan. God wants a right heart but he also wants a right plan. Most great men of God have made breaks from the world. Start working and you will see action in your Christian life. Our goal and prayer for 1985 is to see 100 works, 400 leaders and 15,000 workers established on

many major United States campuses. By the year 2000:
10,000 workers, 50,000 leaders and two million workers.
These are conservative figures. More should happen as we
grow in humility and grace.

What is the most important thing for a child? To be a
part of a family. God's will for us is to be a part of a
family. We have to honour our parents (our church
leaders) and love our brothers and sisters (church
colleagues). A leg must have a body and a body a head.
Our head is Jesus. If we get isolated this may mean
spiritual death. The most important thing for any soldier is
an army.

I'd rather be a failure for God than a success in the
world. We must be determined and disciplined to practice
what we know. We must share the Gospel and serve others
more and take every moment to serve and share. The road
to maturity is testing and we must gain experiential
knowledge of God. The day we go with the majority is the
day we stop walking with Christ. Satan will give us
something good that will make us miss the best. Our
companions should be those who fear the Lord. But we
must have compassion towards unbelievers and not think
we have all the truth. We must put new wine in new
wineskins and form new churches.

According to the *CAUSE,* December 1982, an article
about this conference said, "There were many new
Christians who came, who had never heard God's will laid
out so clearly. We're confident...that a good number were
linked up with us as a result of what they both heard and
saw". The messages I heard that weekend were tough. I
was a little bewildered by the whole event. People were
yelling amens and there were tears of joy. It was an
emotional, busy, giant pep rally to motivate the troops. The
sermons brought together all the same messaging we had
been getting from our own Elders. We left the conference

with renewed energy to continue with our work. I believed that the work of this church would be my life.

August and September 1982 were hopping with activities. There was always our evangelism outreach, our meetings plus the extra curricular activities our BDG did together. Ours was the single's BDG and we did everything from collecting vegetables that were destined to be thrown out at the research station, to attending Christian rock concerts in the Big City. We also liked to paint Christian messages on the campus billboard set aside for that purpose. Many students hated the *Bible* verses and we thought it was fun to see how long a message could last before it was painted over or graffitied. In addition to our work on campus we also did outreach by going door to door or visiting nearby parks. Then there were our university contacts from the surveys. These were of highest priority and we had to be diligent in following up on as many as possible.

That fall I had been working on my own stack of survey results with the names of women students, who lived in residence and indicated they were open to learning more about the *Bible*. They had filled out the same surveys that I did just two years ago. Beth and I went out to meet the students and the more we did that, the larger the gap appeared between myself and them even though I was only a student myself just four months ago. I felt I was living in an entirely different world.

One of the students we visited often was Ann. Sometimes I would go visit her without Beth and when we were alone, she would open up and confide in me. She had a girlfriend who was picking on her because she said she did not agree with the Theory of Evolution. We both felt that there may be a better explanation, not yet discovered, because the scientific proof was just not there. Together we practised our elevator speeches on this topic and researched scripture verses that could support our beliefs. We both knew what kind of persecution to expect given that I had graduated in a science major and she too was studying science.

Sometimes Ann would have her friends over and I would laugh and joke with them for a little while. Ann and I couldn't talk about Christianity forever and certainly not with her friends present. However when the topic of discussion was not about religious matters, I found myself feeling awkward. One of the friends was in love with two different guys who lived in the same residence and could not decide which one to choose. She was unhappy because the situation had become very complicated. Everyone had advice for her but what could I say? Should I tell her that these discussions were frivolous in the big picture of what was happening in the world. Should I tell her spending so much time with men you had no intention of marrying, was a waste of time. I chose to remain silent.

I felt these friends would not understand my point of view because they were not Christians. They invited me out on many occasions for pizza and beer on Thursday nights. I made excuses why I could not go. Thursday nights had become evangelism nights. When asked out to the dances and lounges, I just could not go. I did not want to get pulled into the world's way of thinking and behaving. The church called it backsliding into sin. I knew that even too much laughter was a problem because I could say something that I really did not mean or it could tarnish my Christian witness. Life was serious and I had important work to do for God. I could not be friends with my contacts and we lived in very different worlds.

I was content with my new life in that I did not feel guilty all the time. I had been forgiven and I was at peace with myself. Getting to know my Creator and His will for my life was exciting and joy filled. I felt I had been showered with a million graces. I had so many fiends in my life to learn from and pattern myself after in a way that was pleasing to God. Yet there was something missing. I don't know why I had become so calculating in everything I said or did. I had to run everything through my system of priorities and think before I acted. Thursday night's Pizza and beer would have been a great way to relax and enjoy my new friends. I missed being spontaneous. I missed the old me.

Somehow I wished I could have this great relationship with God but go back in time and start over. If only I could go back to the day I first arrived on this campus, so far from home, and still have my faith, my old life and my old friends, in addition to the new ones. I had become a goldfish in a bowl looking out at life. Something was wrong and I had changed in ways that I did not like and that terrified me. So I prayed for answers. I prayed about funding ways to get back in touch with people not connected with the church.

I confided in Jason, one of the senior brothers who echoed the same concerns I had. He too was trying to connect with people outside the church. I know Kari was also feeling like a goldfish. She had started to drop church activities and replace them with various sports clubs at the university. Beth became upset that Kari was missing meetings and she asked the Elders to intervene. They met with Kari and discouraged her from spending time with people outside the church. They told her she needed to get her life back on track. Even though this involved someone I was close to and lived with, I only learned about this from the bits and pieces that were said to me or I picked up from other people's conversations.

Wherever a problem arose in the church, the leadership always jumped in to sort things out quickly and quietly. Beth told me issues were handled that way so that other members would not get distracted by the drama. I was also told that UBS did not condone gossip and if something did not directly involve you, it was none of your business. The grapevine was still active but the information was shared discreetly so as to not get caught. Sharing what you heard was discouraged. If the responsible senior brothers and sisters could not deal with the problem effectively, the Elders were called in. Problems always took on a very serious tone if the Elders had to be involved. Elders were kept apprised of the progress within every household. Beth had regular meetings with Ron to report back about Kari, Donna and I.

I was incredibly busy. Every moment was devoted to the goals of the church, so much so that I started to get really tired. In fact I became worn down, exhausted and ended up with chronic bronchitis followed by the worst influenza I had ever experienced. I was bedridden for three days. We were taught to run hard for Christ like the disciples did. I had doubts however about the pace of what I was doing. God would not expect me to work so hard that I made myself sick. I reflected on my notes from the summer conference and saw how the messaging had pushed me to work more than I should have. The messaging was based on a lot of what I knew was true. However on closer examination, when I peered into the shadows and took different views from other angles, something was not quite right about the Teachings. I was not sure what.

CHAPTER TEN

Later that fall, Gerry, a professor, researcher and Elder in training, suggested that we travel into the Big City for an outreach excursion, he called a Blitz. There were fifteen of us from our BDG organized into vehicles and vans. We gathered at the designated place in front of a Christian bookstore. From there we were assigned partners and designated street corners. I was paired with my roommate Donna plus Jason and Derrick. We were situated on the city's busiest street corner, just outside a large shopping centre. This was the first time that I did any evangelism with anyone other than Beth and I was happy to be paired with Donna. She was someone I knew fairly well and I was feeling apprehensive.

This was a very unusual day in this city. I had visited it many times but today was different. There were two different demonstrations that stopped traffic as they took over the streets. One was a group of Marxists and the second group was concerned about events related to the European, Israeli and Arab conflict. Plus we ended up sharing the same street corner with five Hare Krishna followers. I had read about them but had never seen them or met them in person before. One sat at a little table while two chanted and played their finger symbols. The remaining two talked to individuals that had gathered round to watch. They were all males with shaved heads except for one pony tail at the back. They were wearing salmon pink pyjama-like outfits. Some of the onlookers were poking fun at them.

We chatted with them off and on throughout the day. They did not seem happy that we were there. At one point I tried to share the Gospel with one of them but was not well received. He just said, "Bless you sister" and then pushed me aside to speak with someone else. As he did that I caught a glimpse of an elderly woman with long straggly grey hair, laying prostrate in front of the shopping mall doors. People were walking in wide circles around her, staring down at her but nobody seemed to be helping her. I went over to see if she was OK.

I had to kneel down on the cement in front of her. Her clothes were badly tattered and dirty and her fingernails were long and bluish in colour. When I spoke to her, she rose to her knees and told me that God told her to do this to protest the worldliness of mankind. I was taken aback because I was there to share the Gospel and instead she was trying to share her faith with me. She told me how God had sent her into the local bars against her own will and now to lay on the sidewalk. I began to think she was mentally unstable. I could not believe that God would force someone into this extreme level of debasement, doing things that were clearly causing self-harm. Something was not right. It was then that a wave of regret washed over me.

I was feeling really uncomfortable when she then looked into my eyes and said, "I know you dear. I know who you are." She began telling me about myself, my inner thoughts and my fears. The hair on the back of my neck stood on end as she described things about myself that only I could possibly know. She talked about the things I had been praying to God about. She described me in the big picture of the world and my spirituality. I knew what she was saying was true but was barely able to grasp it, almost like she was describing things beyond human understanding. She had rejected any discussion about Christ. She would not even acknowledge His name when I spoke. She behaved like she did not hear me.

However She spoke about spiritual matters with authority and it slowly dawned on me that I was not conversing with a human being, but some spirit entity. What kind of spirit was this? Then I came too late, to the realization that this woman may be possessed by a demon or was a demon herself. I thought about how the disciples of Christ cast out demons in His name. I considered it for a very short speck of time and then thought better of it. No, this was something much bigger than anything I was prepared to deal with. I just wanted to get away from her as fast as I could. I felt as if I had come face to face with Satan himself. As I rose to my feet and distanced myself, I was left in awe of the cunning and superior intellect with which the things of God were distorted and used against me. This encounter was not something I could shrug off easily and it haunted me in the years to come.

I had never experienced so many oddities as this day in this city. While I was speaking to the old woman, I could see Donna chatting with a young man. As she spoke to him, he just stared past her the entire time. His arms were crossed and feet spaced apart and planted in the ground. As I moved toward them, I could see that his eyes were dark, his hair long and wavy. He wore a black leather jacket and blue jeans. He had a hard cold look about him and he kept himself at arms length from Donna and I. He was sizing us up and just gave me a cold stare and ignored me when I asked him a question. After that Donna took him over and introduced him to Jason and Derrick.

It was just then when the other teams came to get us. We were done for the day. I was still very spooked by my encounter with the old woman and was so preoccupied by thoughts of what she had said to me, I did not notice that the young man Donna had been talking to, had joined us for supper. After the meal Donna and I went back to Gerry's van for the trip back home. Jason did not return with us but stayed behind with the young man we had met. His name was Grant and Donna and I began praying that he would accept Christ into his life. It turned out that when we arrived home, we saw that Grant had made the decision to join us. He had a conversion experience while with Jason and decided he wanted to learn more. Donna and I were happy that prayers had been answered and started jumping up and down with joy like crazy people.

Diary June 12, 1982: We travelled to the Big City to share the Gospel with many people on a Blitz mission. I passed out a couple of hundred pamphlets. Mark was very open and searching for answers. I gave him a New Testament and shared the Gospel with him. Donna and Jason shared the Gospel with Grant.

...

Diary June 19, 1982: No evangelism tonight. Donna and I paired up tonight and needed to talk instead. We had some things bothering us.

We worked hard to do a lot of evangelizing all summer. The expectations to produce spiritual offspring, as we called them, was great. I wasn't sure where this pressure was coming from or who was driving it. UBS did place a strong emphasis on proselytizing but I wondered if these standards were self inflicted. Maybe I was just trying to prove to myself, Kari, Beth and the church that I had matured as a Christian. As time went on and as we waded into the summer season, I found that a high level of this kind of activity, very difficult to maintain. More and more

I was starting to question the benefits of the cold turkey evangelizing assignments.

> ***Diary June 21, 1982:*** *Lord, I am having a hard time remembering the references for the scripture verses. Please help me remember them. Help me to be more diligent in studying the Word. There is so much I need to learn about loving others, serving others, being others oriented, being perceptive to my own sins and learning wisdom and understanding. Help me to perceive the problems in others lives as well so I can help them. Like Donna, give me the courage or rebuke her out of love.*

As the spring ended and the summer began, Donna and I had grown closer. Donna was not the easiest person to live with. One minute she would be really nice and calm. Then the next minute she would be upset and angry about something that seemed trivial. She had been harbouring anger towards Kari and Beth about something that happened before I came to live with them. It was obvious that whatever it was had not been adequately resolved. Donna was strong willed with matching emotions and mood swings. She was rarely on an even keel. Instead of thinking the best of Donna, I suspected that she had broken the trust of Kari and Beth somehow. I could see that the two older sisters had withdrawn from Donna and no longer confided in her.

I was not allowed to know what happened or what was going on. This was a private matter between my three roommates. Donna was not allowed to tell me about it. I was left to observe and make assumptions. I know Kari and Beth were friends in university and had joined UBS together years ago, long before Donna came on the scene. Donna was a very independent person and living in this household without me, would have made her the odd person out. Donna sensed their aloofness towards her and accused them of not accepting her or acting in a loving manner towards her. On top of that she was continually criticized for committing sins of failing to forgive others and harbouring bitterness towards them. The older sisters told her she needed to get closer to God, that she lacked faith and needed to seek God's strength to deal with her emotions.

From what I saw, Donna was being singled out and not being treated in a loving manner. She felt hurt by this. As I got to know her better, I felt that the church was wrong about her. Donna had studied theology and had a high level of knowledge and had served in leadership positions in other churches before coming to UBS. At the same time I listened to Kari and Beth because I respected them. I was told we were supposed to accept difficulties with a stoic attitude, turn the other cheek and let the issues go. As a result there were no attempts to examine Donna's complaints. I was stuck in the middle and was expected to accept their criticism of Donna. They said Donna needed to be more submissive and learn from her older sisters like I was doing. Donna was being told by the higher ups in the church that her Biblical education amounted to nothing. I believe they were trying to humble her and break her because she had more formal training than the Elders. I felt that they needed to discredit her but I did not know why.

This dispute eventually spilled over into the evangelizing assignments. Kari was no longer happy to be paired with Donna. They could not agree on the approach being taken. Kari wanted to work with Beth again as they had been doing for years. Beth on the other hand was the Head of our household and did not want Donna going out without senior supervision by herself or Kari. Donna and I also wanted to see a change in the assignment. She and I had grown close and we wanted to work together. It took a while but we eventually convinced Beth to agree to the changes. We knew it would make the entire household much happier in the end.

Donna was a wonderful person despite her moods. She was very intelligent and didn't let any unfounded comments slip by without a challenge. You could not quote scripture incorrectly and get away with it because she would check. She had memorized a tremendous amount of scripture and had a photographic memory. She was also quick to set the record straight if she was not pleased about something. Donna kept everyone on their toes and was a problem for anyone who considered themselves to be in a position of power. I believe she was greatly misunderstood, underestimated and undervalued. She was often the target of correction from the Elders and frequently appeared stressed, confused and emotional.

Kari too started to become a bit unhinged. Within our BDC we now had equal numbers of single men and women and we started evangelizing together. Through this new configuration, Kari had the opportunity to meet and spend time with George. He started bringing home baked pies to our house and Kari confided in me that she and George had fallen for each other. Suspicious, Beth and Donna demanded details about the relationship. Kari would not let on to them that it was anything more than a casual friendship. I knew differently but kept her secret and supported her. The others didn't and I could hear the heated arguing, behind closed doors between Kari, Beth and Donna. Again, I was not allowed to be a part of these discussions and nobody would tell me any details.

George was a new recruit to our church. I did learn that the relationship between Kari and George was causing problems among the singles of the church. One person's selfish desires had to take a back seat to that. Therefore anything that became a distraction to the members of the church was to be discouraged or cut out. Beth told me it was not appropriate for one of the brothers to give special attention to any one sister. What I did know was that Kari and George really cared for one another. Kari's face lit up when George was around. I had never seen her so happy.

A quick move towards marriage would solve the issue in my opinion. Both Kari and George were in their late twenties and early thirties respectively. The nonsense of puppy love was not what this relationship was about. These were two very stable mature people. I was under the impression that Kari and George were seeking the blessing of the Elders to pursue something more serious and squash the rumours and unrest within the singles group. I was waiting for good news and got the impression from Kari that talks were going in a direction that she was excited about. I was expecting them to announce their engagement.

Instead Beth and Donna went to the Elders about the issue of George. What happened after that was unexpected. The three Elders agreed to ban George from visiting our apartment. I was bewildered and confused. The general opinion I picked up through eavesdropping, was that George was just a new Christian and was not mature or committed enough yet to understand the higher goals of the church. There were other more senior single men that would be better suited to Kari in terms of their training in Christ. I was so disappointed for Kari. I could hear her crying in her room, behind a closed door, for days.

When Kari finally did emerge from her room to face the rest of us, it was as if the light in her eyes had been extinguished. She and George were not allowed to see each other anymore. All she would tell me was that everything was fine and that the Elders knew what was best for her. She felt God was watching over her through them. Kari swallowed her pride and carried on. The relationship that started with so much joy and hope ended quickly in ruin and heartbreak. Shortly after that George left the church.

This was all so very confusing for me. I was not aware

of the implications this event would have on the future direction of my own life. I had accepted that if someone had asked for the Elders advice in a personal matter, they would probably be wise to follow it. However, I was not so sure why anyone would even involve them in such personal matters. I wondered why Kari even went to them in the first place. If she had just let things flow naturally and not put so much weight on the opinions of the Elders, perhaps she and George would have still been together. When it came to matters of love and marriage this was absolutely something far too serious a decision to put in the hands of someone else. Our personal lives were none of their business, so I thought.

As the end of the fall season descended on me, I felt as if a cloak of darkness had covered me. It had either just befallen me or had been there for some time and I had only just awakened to its presence. I am not sure which case was true but my summer of dedication to the church, in search of knowledge brought me more questions than answers. Not only was I feeling heavy, it was as if a large cloud of fog had separated me from God. Something was not right. The clear and simple joy of the relationship that I had in the beginning of my conversion, seemed to be slipping away. To combat this I prayed more, did more evangelism and read more scripture as I was told I needed to do.

My difficulties arose from the fact that I was supposedly a knowledgeable Christian going out to teach people about Christ. I was the one with something to share and information to impart, to challenge people to return to God. The reality was much different than this. What was actually happening was the reverse of this. Everyone I talked to taught me something new. Instead of me teaching people about God. God was using every new contact to teach me instead. I was always the party that ended up being encouraged in my faith. Was I doing something

113

wrong or was I not meant to do this kind of Christian work? Given what happened to Kari, I chose to keep these doubts to myself.

There was one particular Saturday afternoon I will never forget. I had wandered downtown to do some shopping. I took the bus and when I got off, I was really hoping to run into someone I knew. I felt lost and did not know what to do with myself. I was extremely uncomfortable, nervous and had trouble deciding where to go. An alarm bell was going off. This was a moment in time that etched deep into my memory when I realized that I had not been alone for a single waking moment in the past four months. Twenty four hours a day, seven days a week I had been in the company of others at work, at church activities and in my home. When I was not at work or a church event, Kari and Beth planned every minute in between.

It was not as if I was easily led and just chose to go along with the crowd. I liked doing the things my roommates planned out for us. I was not one to plan out my leisure activities ahead of time. I preferred to be spontaneous about my free time and see what I felt like doing in that moment. In our household, everything was planned ahead and if I wanted to change the plans I had to come up with something ahead of time to replace that empty time slot. This was just futile. I could not say, I wanted to do nothing. They would say there is no such thing. Plus when I first came to university here, this part of the country was new to me. My roommates knew the area and were really good at introducing me to the sights.

I had already started questioning and wondering about my role in the church and the validity of the evangelism outreach we were doing. By the end of summer I was still left asking myself for the umpteenth time, if this cold turkey evangelism was something I should be doing. At this point in the season I had spoken to over thirty women and nobody was saved or converted, from what I could tell. No amount of prayer seemed to be affecting the desired outcome. I was not alone. I overheard Kari having a conversation about his very topic. After that I found out they had a special meeting to discuss Kari's problems where they admonished her to continue the work.

When the alarm went off about never being alone, I knew that I was experiencing some sort of withdrawal and mental distress from the church. This caused me to question my life with UBS. What would my future with them look like? Was there even a role for me other than wife and mother. I had more to offer. That is not how I ever imagined my future. All the leaders were men and women could not teach scripture to men. Our Teachings for Women Class was being taught by Jeff. This was ridiculous and embarrassing. There were rumours of various senior women taking over, but nobody stepped up. I was too low in the hierarchy. The Elders said that they supported women in leadership positions. However the teachings taught us to be submissive and this did not bode well for my hope of a feminine leadership.

This past September, our BDG decided to help the students move into residence. I took the lead and made all the arrangements to obtain the necessary permissions from the university. When I reported this to the Elders, Ron said I should not be doing this and he delegated one of the male leaders in our BDG, to take over what I was doing. I was not happy about this and felt that I was being put in my place as a woman and a newer member of the church. To appease my disappointment and help me grow in responsibility, I was given another task. I was now in charge of organizing the pot luck meals at the weekly Sunday night Breaking of Bread.

I began to feel hopeless, helpless and frustrated. I chose

not to dwell on this but I was becoming apathetic about my worth and potential contribution in the world. I was hoping that this was all a misunderstanding. Perhaps if the right woman came along, the leadership would change? Maybe I could be that woman? I was certainly primed for it and had self confidence. However I could not just step into a new church and expect to lead when there were so many long timers who were seasoned and experienced. I was irritated and impatient with the inaction of my sisters. My Saturday excursion alone downtown, woke me up to the realization that this church and my situation in it, was just too close for comfort.

CHAPTER ELEVEN

It was later that fall, when I was fully immersed in church activities, that I noticed Grant. He was one of the new recruits we had met during a Blitz. He was in our BDG singles group and lived in Jason's household. I took an interest in him because he was full of life, confident and non-conforming. That was the opposite to how I had been feeling about myself lately. He said and did whatever he thought was right, regardless of what others were doing, thinking or telling him to do. Many church members did not like him and could not look beyond his rough exterior. They thought he was a rebel in dire need of more church Teachings and the guidance of the senior brothers. They tolerated him because he was considered a baby in Christ. I, on the other hand, thought he was wonderful. I saw him as a breath of fresh air in my increasingly stale life.

Grant loved to do crazy things. He liked to think outside the box. He dominated the meetings with enthusiasm and new ideas. Sometimes he would bring alternative Christian music on a portable stereo player, to spruce up a dull prayer meeting. He frequently offered to play drums to accompany guitars at the Sunday morning teachings. He even started writing his own songs. At one point he offered to make a film about the church to promote it. He was a doer that put one hundred percent of himself into everything he did. The Elders saw him as potential leadership material but they first had to clip his wings to channel him the right direction, their direction.

One month after my first Blitz to the Big City, our BDG planned another outreach. This time we were travelling to a steel producing city to the south of us. This city was not as big but it had a large university. The older married members of our BDG did not come with us this time. This excursion was for singles only. When we arrived we were paired up, male and female for safety. After all the couples were matched, only Grant and I were left. Over the past month since Grant's arrival, I had never spoken to him. I had only watched him from across the room. Now, I was glad for the opportunity to get to know him.

Grant and I were assigned to the core of the city across from a small park area. We mostly handed out the little pamphlets. We talked to all kinds of people but mostly just small talk. Nobody wanted to engage with us enough for us to share our Gospel message. Most of the people were exiting a small shopping mall and just hurried past us. It did not take us long to run out of our reading material, so we moved to the park. The people sitting leisurely on the park benches, seemed much more open to having a discussion with us.

Tired of talking, we sat down to take a break on a bench next to an elderly couple. They had been watching us for a long time and initiated a conversation with us. They told us how they had been missionaries most of their lives. They described all the places in the world where they had worked. The number of places and the large geographic footprint of their mission covered most of the world. I was rather amazed at the ground they had covered in their lifetime. Then they described with great detail the spiritual condition of the people inhabiting many locations around the world. I remember they were most urgently concerned for the souls of the people living in France and Los Angeles. Their story was absolutely fascinating and we spoke for a long time. Here I was once again, at the receiving end of God's teaching.

Eventually the conversation turned to us and the couple asked about our future plans. They asked outright if they were getting married and planning to be missionaries ourselves. I was embarrassed by the question because this was the first time Grant and I had even been together alone. We did not even know each other. They were very adamant and spoke with authority about their opinion that we should get married. They encouraged us to continue with the work we were doing and said they thought we worked well together.

Shortly after we finished talking to the elderly couple, we left to do some shopping. Together we wondered out loud about the interesting discussion we just had. We believed they were missionaries because they were intent on sharing their faith with us. However we could not believe they could cover so many miles in one lifetime and know so much about the spiritual condition of so many people. That was astounding. This couple must have been hundreds of years old to have accomplished all they described. Then Grant and I went silent, looked at each other and both said, "Maybe they were angels?" Then I thought to myself, "Did they know something about Grant and I that we didn't? Were they prophesying our future marriage?" Then we both quickly changed the topic on our uncomfortable silent musings.

One evening, weeks later, my roommate failed to show up for our evangelism assignment. I was looking for a partner so I called Jason's wife and asked her to go with me. She couldn't come but Grant was at her house and he overheard the conversation and offered to accompany me. As a rule men and women do not go out on evangelism together. However Grant and I worked well together during the last outreach Blitz. I could not see any reason not to do it again. Plus I wanted to get to know him more and enjoyed his company. I accepted his offer.

Grant and I walked around campus talking to people about Christ. Between these discussions we shared our life stories. He was easy to talk to. Neither of us felt we could share our past lives with others in the church. Most seemed reluctant to discuss their history and that made it hard to know and trust them. I had assumed many of them grew up in Christian homes and led ultra sheltered lives. This of course was an incorrect assumption. However, on this one particular evening, being able to relax, let down our guard and be our true selves, was refreshing. We were both relatively new to the church and it was good to have someone I felt I could relate to.

We had decided that we should go out on evangelism together again but we soon found out that that was not going to happen. The Elders were very unhappy about what we did. Grant's talk of seeing me again had many in the church concerned. Grant had plans to take me to a Christian concert in the Big City and told everyone about it. Grant had taken a liking to me and wanted to pursue a more meaningful friendship. I did not know about this or what he had told others. We had just met and I had only been alone with him on two occasions. Other than a few questions from my roommates about my relationship with Grant, which I told them was non-existent, I had no idea what kind of stir was taking place.

Grant never had the chance to even ask me out to the concert because that was intercepted by a meeting with one of the Elders. Ron asked me to meet him for lunch at the office in the Student Union building. This was like being

120

called to the principal's office in grade school. Ron wanted to know what was going on with Grant. I told him the same thing I told my roommates. Ron then informed me about the nixed concert invitation from Grant. Jason had put a stop to it by telling Grant he could not do that. I was actually quite pleased to learn that Grant wanted to ask me out. I tried to hide my pleasure at this news. I smiled and told Ron that I did find Grant attractive.

Ron was very serious and was not amused by my attempt to lighten the mood. He informed me that dating was not allowed and was only sanctioned for couples that had been given permission to be engaged, when the date of the wedding was close. I was a little bit in shock. This was the first time I had heard about this, in my almost two years of involvement in the church. My mind was screaming What!!! I was feeling a mixture of disbelief and anger. This was too strict. It was unreasonable. The church had crossed a line, a personal boundary. I could not find the words to defend my position in the avalanche of emotions that were taking over. Why are people not told about this before joining UBS?

Ron could probably sense my frustration and that I had shut down. He went on to explain the church's rules regarding marriage. My mind had gone into an angry inner dialogue with myself saying, "I had voluntarily signed up for UBS. They have no jurisdiction over the private and personal matters of my life." Meanwhile all I was hearing from Ron was blah, blah blah. It seems the Elders did not want the church disrupted by the problems that go along with courting, breakups and jealousy. The rule was to prevent young people from being tempted by sin. They felt that a single person should be able to do the work of God undistracted from their goals. If it was God's will that a couple should be together, then this could be worked out quickly, quietly and privately.

I protested my indignation of only learning about this rule now. Ron explained that new recruits were not informed. They were not at a point in their spiritual lives, where they could understand and appreciate this directive. He continued on saying that a couple that was considering marriage, needed to ask the advice of the Elders before making any plans. As his lips kept moving my mind was swimming and telling me that this discussion about marriage was premature. I had not even thought about Grant in a serious way. Marriage was the last thought on my mind. I was embarrassed when the elderly couple talked about it on our Blitz and now the same uncomfortable conversation was happening again! This must be a message that God was trying to clobber me over the head with. However, was it "You must marry Grant!" or "You must stay away from Grant!" I was not sure but my heart was leaning towards the former.

Ron continued talking, knowing I was only half listening to him. He seemed to get more intense as time dragged on. He asked me to think about other men in the church that I would like to marry other than Grant. Then he tried to warn me about Grant saying he could not be trusted. He sunk even deeper by telling me about the wiles of men, sexuality and how men could not be trusted. Wow! I thought, "How dare he!" This discussion was absurd. Did he think I was a child? I was twenty five years old and had been living on my own for seven years. I was indignant and said to myself, "Who did he think he was interfering with my life in such a personal way?"

I walked away from this meeting with a new perspective. A chord of rebellion had been struck inside of me. I started to feel alive again even if it was ignited by anger. The positive take away was that I was pleased that Grant was interested in me because I liked him too. It was as simple as that. We did not go out on evangelism or go on any dates. We stayed away from each other as directed.

We just simply looked for each other at opposite ends of the room in every meeting we attended. We were constantly aware of each other's presence.

Eventually Grant moved into Jason's household. To help them celebrate, I baked them a cherry pie. I should say I baked Grant a cherry pie. The fact that others would share it, did not interest me. To thank me for the pie, Grant wrote me a note that was passed to me by one of the sisters. The letter invited further correspondence so I wrote him back and found a trusted hand to deliver the message on my behalf. Grant responded to my letter and soon we were writing back and forth through our designated couriers. We wrote often and faithfully for months. It was through our letters that the relationship, everyone was trying to stop, blossomed. We were falling in love but nobody was allowed to know. It was an underground relationship built on mutual sharing with a bond that grew deep and solid.

Although we did not ever see each other in person and tried hard to hide our feelings at meetings, the Elders continued to pursue us. Obviously our trusted couriers were spies. They would not be satisfied with our discretion. We were not distracting anyone and we had not missed any meetings. We had followed the Elder's advice. We did not see or talk to one another in person. Plus we were continuing with the work of the church, undisturbed by the letter writing. Was this not what we were asked to do? We were following the rules. What could go wrong?

CHAPTER TWELVE

Diary August 22, 1982: Dear Lord, please show me if I am obeying You and heeding Your advice or the advice of the Elders and show me my disobedience. I confess that I am partial to Grant but show me how I am doing that in a way that I shouldn't be. I guess by sending him letters I am doing that very thing. I won't give him this letter today if you don't want me to. Show me what to do and cause me to be obedient to You because I think I might not be doing that based on how people are reacting to me. Help me to see what is happening more clearly.

Diary August 26, 1982: Dear Lord You said we would be free in Christ but I have been feeling burdened by the dos and don'ts ever since I became a committed Christian. I do not think this is what You want...I want to be free from the rules but at the same time I want to know You in me, apart from just head knowledge given to me by others. Please help me to discover who You are for myself and to know completely what this relationship is and what You have planned for me. Please guide me as I try to find freedom in You. I may be a little reckless but I fully commit my life into Your hands. Based on this I am just going to do what seems best to me without calculating, pondering or stressing-out and overthinking everything. I am just going to determine what speaks to my heart as being the right thing to do. Lord, please help me therefore be able to distinguish between Your Spirit in me and a deceitful heart. I ask you to intervene when I am deceived.

Grant and I simply had a good friendship. An innocent friendship. Was that so bad? I did want to do what God wanted me to. He loves me and knows what is best. This whole thing with Grant had caused me to pray even more fervently. I was not even sure if I ever wanted to get married or if that was in the future plans for me. The Elders had taught us that it is better to be single and I wanted to know if this friendship with Grant should continue or not. Perhaps he was distracting from something else I should be focused on? The *Old Testament* says that the heart can be deceitful above all else. Even though I felt Grant was a good person, was this friendship with Grant a ruse to redirect me away from something better? If Grant was a stumbling block for me, I prayed that God would take it away.

Diary August 28, 1982: It was nice that Grant and I could spend some time together. I want to commit our relationship to You. I want to leave it up to You, Lord, if and when we should see each other. I know that yesterday was planned for us.

I could not believe that such a big deal was being made about an innocent friendship. I had not even thought about the physical aspect of the relationship. We had not even had the urge to hold hands. Our relationship had only grown through letter writing. However it was important to the Elders that every member was fruitful by spending more time reading the Word and sharing our faith. A Christian was considered fruitful if your outreach brought new disciples into the church. We were told to commit our ways to God, have undistracted devotion to Him, to bear our crosses and deny ourselves for the sake of the Gospel. We were also told to put the needs of others ahead of our own (*Philippians* 2:3-4) and that love is patient and does not seek its own (1 *Corinthians* 13:4-7).

For every action and decision that was made, there was a scripture verse to go with it. My mind was overloaded with so many Bible verses that I had to sort through, every time I did something. Now I had a new set of rules to add to the mountainous pile already stewing in every corner of my mind. At first I thought if I just ignored the Elders and physically conformed to their rules, the whole issue would go away. However the Elders would not leave us alone. They were relentless. Now I was being made to feel guilty about even writing a simple note to him. All I knew was that the Elders continued to push the issue because of what they believed about the nature of our relationship. Grant and I were requested, again, to meet with the Elders. This one such meeting was particularly brutal.

Diary October 6, 1982: Ron asked Grant and I to meet with him together in the Student Union building. When we arrived, we found we had been ambushed because Jeff and Beth were also there.

John opened the meeting by saying, "We've really prayed about this and your relationship with one another. I hope you will realize that we asked you to come here because we love you and want to see the best things happen. I would suggest that the both of you spend time in the Word and get convictions from the Word regarding what is best for your life. We have already asked that you not see each other, however you shouldn't necessarily set a time limit on how long you should not talk to each other anymore. But you could suggest a time period that I would like to see, for at least one year. You could set standards ahead of time so you won't have to decide at each opportunity what you need to do to achieve this so you

127

won't be swayed. You could periodically evaluate the relationship but you shouldn't think about it very much. You should set standards in accordance with the times you know you shouldn't be together. You must cut those meeting times completely."

Ron said, "You are just teasing one another. In order to be sure you are really meant for one another you should stop seeing each other completely for a period of time. You'll have to cool it until we set a time for re-evaluation."

Beth added, "You must stop having the kind of relationship you now have."

The no dating policy was meant to be beneficial to the furtherance of the Gospel, for the glory of God. Grant and I were told not to see each other and we did not. The Elders told us that if we really cared for one another we would do what was best for the other. This was mostly directed at me because I was considered the more mature Christian. I was told that I needed to back off so Grant could get the chance to be more grounded in scripture, even though I was not the initiator in any of this. In the beginning, I just ignored all the concern about nothing but as time went on I became more and more distressed. They wanted us to build a mental and emotional wall between us. I believe they wanted to control my heart and break my spirit.

Grant was given a little booklet called *How Should a Christian Date* by Henry Hintermeister. I was not given a copy of it and did not see it until Grant showed it to me months later. The booklet outlined the problems of dating, the purpose of the single life and God's guidelines for interaction. According to Hintermeister, dating is problematic because it prevents us from being wholly devoted to others and it makes provision for fleshly desires. He says that the purpose of the single life is to be free to delight ourselves in the Lord and spend time alone with the Lord. As a single, we must learn moral purity, financial stability, dependability and surround ourselves with friends of the same sex. He said we need to be free in our single-hood to develop the right attitudes towards authority because rebellion is one of the most common sins of our day.

This summarizes what Hintermeister and UBS believed was the process to marriage that replaced dating:

1. Pray for a partner and seek council in the *Bible* and from your leaders
2. Let the peace of God rest in your heart on the matter
3. Be sensitive and aware of God's timing
4. The man must make the first move, not the woman* only after the following is established:
   - Confidence in God's leading
   - Surety of God's timing
   - Surety of one's own Christian development
   - Confidence in the woman's Christian development
   - Agreement from parents and leaders
5. Communicate the desire for marriage with the woman while remaining open to her decision to say no

* If the woman makes the first move God's order of the man taking the spiritual initiative is upset. Beware of the woman who takes matters into her own hands! She will not stop doing this once she is married. There is a lifetime of struggle ahead unless she breaks before God. - Hintermeister

I continued to be disturbed about the fact that I was never told about this rule and many others. I was discovering them as time went on, and was not fully informed when I was first interviewed by the Elders and agreed to join the UBS household. I challenged Beth about this and wanted to know why she, of all people, did not tell me all the expectations, policies and practices up front. She said I was not ready to hear these things at that time. I told her that I was going to tell all our new recruits about these secrets. She warned me not to tell them because they were not mature and committed enough to handle it.

Grant and I were now forbidden to see each other for a year. It was unclear if I could speak to him. There was some mention of putting a time limit on our discussions. However in the end I was made to understand that not seeing him meant no time alone, no talking alone, no phone calls and no letters. If we wanted to know how the other was doing, we would have asked one of the other brothers or sisters. I had more or less adopted my own dating policy years before UBS. I always maintained that if I did not see that the person I was dating was someone I would spend my life with, it was best to end the relationship sooner than later. A dead end relationship as a ruse to entertain one another was a waste of time in my eyes.

This edict from the Elders was very different and I was very upset about it. I wanted to do what was best for myself. Why wouldn't I? I was a grown woman being told by a bunch of men who did not even know me, that I could not be friends with someone of the opposite sex. There were lots of male and female friendships within the church but not for me. This advice, that I did not solicit in the first place, was harsh and extreme and was unduly interfering with my sense of freedom and free will. Despite my feelings about this, I did try to do what they asked and it was very difficult.

Diary September 9, 1982: Lord, thank you for the advice and counsel of the Elders. They say it is best that I

130

don't spend time with Grant. If this is Your will and it is what is best, please help me to be obedient to that. Please take this burden for me and help me get my priorities straight.

Diary September 10, 1982: *I had been scolded by one of the professors in my department, for not obeying the Elders. Thank you Lord, for humbling me by showing my wickedness. I have been suffering a lack of devotion to you by thinking about Grant and a lack of conviction about the goals of the church...my lack of fanaticism. Help me be obedient when You show me through my Elders, that I am not to spend time with Grant. Please do not let me be a stumbling block to him as I was warned I would be.*

Diary September 15, 1982: *Lord, thank you for showing me that by accepting and listening to the counsel of the Elders, I will be wiser.*

Grant did not accept the advice, attempted to circumvent the rules and tried making plans to see me. I told him to leave me alone and I did my best to avoid him. I was told that I was distracting him and not the other way around. They said he was leadership material for the church and needed to grow in his faith unfettered by me. The difficulties were compounded by the fact we were in the same BDG that met on the average of four to five times a week. We both worked at the university and had the same work hours therefore would pass each other on campus sometimes four times a day. We had the same group of friends in the church and spent all our free time with these same friends.

I wasn't seeing Grant as per the instructions so I could have more time to be devoted to God. The Elders however failed to tell us how not to see each other. What did seeing entail? We took part in the same events and experiences shared by the entire group. We were always physically together at every church meeting, despite the edict of the Elders. It was really uncomfortable to be very selective in who I spoke to and where I moved in the room. The BDG went on a camping trip and in the presence of everyone, Grant and I slipped up and spoke to each other while putting up a tent. Later when everyone was hiking, we spoke to each other, with others around us. Later we were again told we were spending too much time together. This was insanity.

However even when we did not speak, we were always aware of the other's presence in the room. We watched each other interacting with others while distanced. We were always together no matter what, even if it was just in our own hearts and minds through intention. Yes, we had become stumbling blocks for each other. The admiration I had for him in the beginning, when I first saw him at church meetings, the few times we were alone together and the letter writing early on, could not be reversed. Now seeing him all the time, at a distance, across a crowded room, when our eyes met my heart would leap for joy. I had, despite everything, fallen in love with him and he with me.

Diary September 18, 1982: Lord, thank you for the chance to help Grant at his place of work and letting me find out how he is doing.

Diary September 26, 1982: Lord, right now I can't think of anyone else in the world I would rather marry than Grant. This is my heart's desire.

To combat this I threw myself into the new schedule set for us that fall. On Mondays I went out to evangelism with Donna or two of the new recruits Helen and Cheryl. I kept myself very busy and did not see Grant so I could be more devoted to God. However, hardening my heart and blocking out my love for Grant, blocked out the love I had

132

for everything else. I was feeling so oppressed and burdened by the ever mounting pile of rules that it became unbearable. That hard shell I was creating inside me became the biggest obstacle of all in my relationship to Christ and everyone else.

This was not working. I tried to close Grant out of my life but when I did, I closed out God as well. My heart was becoming cold from continually rejecting Grant and that made it almost impossible for me to pray. When I blocked out Grant, I blocked out God. I could not love God without also loving Grant and everyone else. I was so stressed by trying to follow the Elders counsel, that I couldn't concentrate on anything. All I could do was pray to God for help over and over. I wanted to be obedient but what they were asking was just not possible. Even after petitioning God for strength, I could not do it. I begged God to take Grant away from me and He did not. I asked God to make Grant obey the counsel and that had not happened. I was so confused. Perhaps my prayers had been answered but not in the way I was expecting.

Diary September 20, 1982: Lord, help me to discern adulterers from sincere Godly people. Please don't let my emotions sway me from everything You have shown me to be the best way...You know how many times I have been like a little bird in a snare, please don't let it happen.

It really bothered me that Grant was not well liked because he was not as refined as the other seasoned Christians. Actually, It may have been intentional on his part. He resisted conforming to the behaviours expected of him. He fiercely clung to who he was. He also wore long hair, tight jeans and a leather jacket. He looked like the rebel he was but that did not mean he deserved to be rejected in a church that preached God's love. It hurt me to see him sitting by himself when we were in the same room. Often I too sat alone. Many of the women had not warmed up to me either. I was always just the new Christian and Beth and Kari's new recruit. Nobody really tried to get to know me and Kari and Beth always played the role of older sisters, advising and judging me. Donna was the only friend with which I felt we could share an equal footing.

I struggled with this so much that I was having anxiety attacks and nightmares. I had decided that I had enough of this. While praying on the way to work one morning I heard God very clearly telling me to just trust Him. He told me to stop struggling with this myself and give the problem to Him, then trust that He would look after it. Afterwards, I felt strangely calm and finally understood what it meant to give your troubles to God. I had to actually pass the problem over and let go of it, knowing it was in good hands.

I realized that trusting God was like a child trusting her parents. A child did not worry about food on the table, rent and clothing, the parents did that. The child's only concern was to play, learn, be happy and enjoy life. I was finally able to see myself doing this and trusting God. Going forward, I decided that I was not going to worry and concern myself with Elder's advice anymore. It was in God's hands. I asked God to protect me from making any wrong decisions about Grant and about the direction of my life. Whatever happened would be God's will and I would let things just take their natural course according to what I felt in my heart was right. I was done with worry and as a result, I felt the peace of Christ take hold in me like it never had before.

The Elders had not been successful in separating us as much as they hoped. I believe they wanted our unquestioning obedience and Grant was a wildcard so they focused on me. I too was a bit head-strong, as my mother used to say. I had never been able to blindly accept something I was told unless I could understand it for

134

myself. I knew that they were unhappy with us and that they would become even more unhappy going forward, given my new sense of peace and direction. Not seeing Grant and being his friend was wrong. I started writing to Grant again through Donna. I would trust Christ.

Letter to Grant: Dear Grant, It says in John 8:32, "...and you shall know the truth and the truth shall make you free." If Jesus came to free me, and He has freed me, then why do I feel like I am in prison?..When I am afraid of being hurt, I build this little wall around my heart and it turns to stone...I thought I could block you out...but when I harden my heart, it also becomes hard towards Christ and I block Him out too...I am tired of trying not to respond to your letters and writing you when I really want to. I feel freer doing this.

The Elders had another meeting with Grant and I about the importance of setting priorities. I was secretly hoping they would eventually see that Grant and I were meant to be together. Instead the advice was even more negative about our hope for a relationship. The words were not very uplifting. In fact I believe that they were downright nasty. They say you don't really know someone until they become angry and what is inside comes spewing out. I had been the bird in a snare for some time.

Diary November 30, 1982: Ron reminded me, "You are just a new Christian (even though I had been in the church more than two years now) and both you and Grant have a lot of growing to do before you would ever be ready for a relationship with one another. You must, most importantly, learn to admonish others and work at growing closer to the girls in your household. They are your support system".

John said to Grant, "You must learn to seek and follow advice. When you talk to others you must make sure people understand what you say to them because telling half-truths is the same as lying. I want you to grow close to Jason. You also need to learn to handle more than one task at a time, especially if you are thinking about marriage and having a family. You can't just bulldoze ahead with one project at any cost and neglect everything else you have been doing."

CHAPTER THIRTEEN

My position at the university as a laboratory technician, was a nine to five position in a lab, near the older section of campus. The building that houses the lab was made of stone and there were a series of outdated climate controlled rooms in the lower level. That is where I would grow plants and study the pests that attacked them. In some rooms there were potato beetles on potato plants, in others there were root maggots on turnips. All the rooms and the building for that matter, was infested with cockroaches that ate everything they could including my wax markers for the petri dishes. We could not use pesticides to get rid of them because it would have killed the pests we were studying. I had to scare them away every time I went into the lockups. It was not very pleasant.

On the next level up was the first floor, where the department's administration staff were located. Eileen was a secretary for our department. All staff were expected to attend the department's alumni picnic. It was at that event where I first met Eileen and when our friendship began. She was very friendly and talkative and she told me that Christianity was an important part of her life since she was a child. I found out that she loved to talk about life in

137

relation to God, scripture and the practical working out of one's Christian faith. Because she was a professed Christian I began to trust her. She was the first friend I had, outside of UBS, in what seemed like a long time.

Eileen was not much older than me but she had lived a big life, experienced a lot and seemed to have a rare wisdom that I was attracted to. Both she and her husband were Baptists, had five children and the two youngest were twins. Her husband Stuart had graduated from Bible College many years ago before exploring various careers. Sometimes she would invite me over to her house where we would talk for hours until early in the morning. Eileen did most of the talking and she was fascinating to listen to. I cultivated her friendship even though she was not a UBSer. I told her a lot about our church and hoped that she and Stuart would join UBS. Sometime after the friendship started, Stuart came to a Sunday Teaching to check us out. He and Eileen decided not to join our church. Stuart said that Eileen would not be a good fit because of the church's views on the roles of women.

Our Elder in training and professor Gerry, visited Eileen and Stuart in their home one evening. Gerry knew Eileen because he worked in our same department but used my friendship as an excuse to visit her. Gerry talked to Stuart about his role as the head of the household and the head of his wife and children. I was hoping that Stuart had misunderstood something on the Sunday teaching that pushed him away. I was hoping perhaps Gerry could clarify something that would want to make them reconsider joining us. Eileen in particular would be such a great asset. Our church was badly in need of female leadership material. I was learning so much from her.

However the visit had the opposite effect and Stuart was even more convinced that this was not a good fit for them. The admonishment for Stuart to be the head was both an insult and sexist. Gerry was very rude and judged them harshly. I don't know how they expected to recruit new members acting like that. I was very disappointed. Despite this, I remained friends with Eileen. The incident did not dampen our friendship and I was glad for that.

As the summer progressed, Eileen started to notice how stressed out I was becoming. I had been telling her about some of what was happening, but not all. She was a good listener, never judged me and never said anything negative about UBS. She also treated me with respect and would never tell me what to do. Instead she encouraged me to learn on my own. Eileen shared with me a verse from Isaiah and asked me to meditate and pray about this verse over and over for a week. Then after the week I was to tell her what I had found out.

Isaiah 30:15 meditation: In repentance and rest you shall be saved. In quietness and trust is your strength.

The verse strengthened my decision to not worry about all the things the Elders were telling me to do. I told her that going forward, I would just do my best and let whatever happened, happen.

I met Grant one evening coming out of the Athletic Centre. It was already dark and a large number of us were on our way home from the Friday gym night. He asked to talk to me alone for a few minutes. I knew Grant had been away on vacation in the United States and today was his first day back. I wanted to hear how he was doing and I was curious about what he wanted to speak to me about. I choose to ignore the ban. I thought perhaps God had finally taken care of the burden I was carrying. Perhaps my prayer had been answered and Grant was going to end the friendship and make a clean break for the both of us. Grant must have decided to end the persistent torment we had been subjected to. I braced myself, ready to feel the huge weight of worry lifted from me. Now that we had not been seeing each other, and he had gained some distance and perspective, I expected that he finally realized our relationship was a mistake.

We sat on two benches on a walkway that faced one another, just outside the Student Union Building. Grant did not waste any time. I did not get a chance to ask him how he was or about his trip. I was not prepared for what came next. Instead of saying what I expected, Grant began telling me how much I meant to him, that he loved me and that we were meant to be together. In a mental prayer I shot a retort to God saying, "Why are you doing this to me? I thought You were going to help me?" The reply from God was even more sharp and clear. I was stunned. Grant was still talking but I had not heard a word he was saying. I was in a trance as God spoke to me in my mind.

He said, "Wasn't this the one you prayed to Me about?" As I heard His voice in my head, I recalled a prayer from over one and a half years ago, long before Grant joined our church. It was a long prayer of petition that I had forgotten about where I asked God to take my future into His hands. I had asked Him that if He had intended that I marry someday, He would make sure that I would know what to do and would choose the right man. I told Him that looking for a mate was distracting and a nuisance. I did not want to be like other women, always looking for a man. I had neither the time or desire to do that. I asked God to take this task on for me and look after this area of my life for me.

While sitting on this bench across from Grant, that Friday evening, God recalled to my mind every detail of that prayer. I was living in the Navigator household at the time and it was the fall semester of my last year. I had felt a powerful urge to pray and knew that the Holy Spirit had inspired me to do so. The Spirit helped and guided my prayer as I contemplated a future partner. All the characteristics and qualities I needed in a partner were revealed to me. It was like a combined prayer and revelation with new information and insights as I pledged this area of my life into God's care.

On this night, God recalled to my mind all those detailed requirements, visually in my mind like the frames of a film in slow motion. In each frame was a quality I had asked for and how that quality applied to Grant. God showed me that each and everything I had prayed for was right there in front of me, in Grant. When the Lord had finished, I understood why Grant had been so persistent despite the admonishment of the Elders. My mind and heart both knew that Grant and I were destined to be together. I apologized to God for not listening better. I was already in love with Grant and so this was a win all around. My heart knew better than I did. I knew that the Elders had to be wrong somehow and what they were doing to us did not seem right. I had been cherishing a verse that said, "Delight yourself in the Lord and He will give you the desires of your heart" (Psalm 37). I had put my trust in God and Grant was the desire of my heart.

The whole revelation only took seconds. Grant thought I was listening to him. I did not respond to his overtures of love but changed the subject. Neither did I tell him about my conversation with God in those moments. I just held that knowledge in my heart and kept the secret close. I refused to talk to him about marriage or show any interest in him. Now that I knew, I wanted any thoughts of marriage to come from him alone, freely, without any influence from me whatsoever. I did however stop telling him to get lost and leave me alone. I did start spending some time with him, more often and within reason, so as to not raise the hackles of the Elders.

In this private matter between Grant and I, I no longer

141

cared about the opinion of the Elders, my roommates or the others in the church. I knew what God had shown me. It was up to others to come to terms with that. I suspect that those around me sensed I had changed. I had a new found confidence and sense of peace. I felt more grounded and balanced. Plus I felt stronger, armed with a new resolve to challenge the Elders about this. The spark of rebellion that ignited in indignation, the first time I met with Ron about Grant, had been fanned into a full blown fire. However the root cause of those changes would not be what those around me perceived. Having been blinded by judgment and feminine stereotyping, they only saw disobedience, rebelliousness and weakness. As a result, those who should have known me best and did not, my roommates, increased pressure on me to follow the Elder's advice.

However now I felt I could take a stand and I told Beth that I was convinced I should continue my relationship with Grant. I told her that I knew beyond any doubt, that this was God's will for Grant and I. After much discussion and my refusal to budge on the subject, Beth finally backed down. She was surprised at my push back but she did eventually listen to what I was telling her. It was a long time in coming but Beth moved to a middle ground and compromised. I was very pleasantly surprised and pleased by her new position to support me in some capacity. She did not condone what I was doing but did not condemn me either. Donna liked Grant and overall she supported me as well. Kari, who I supported not long ago in her relationship with George, did not support me in any way and condemned me. Kari did not like Grant and neither did Beth.

This very late new found support, gave me a renewed hope, that the Elders would eventually come around to see things my way. After all, if I knew it was God's will, at some point, through all their prayers, would they not also come to the same conclusion? We were both praying to the same God were we not? However, that did not happen. I am not sure we were even praying with the same intent and motive. I was praying about what was best for me but were they? I don't believe so. Instead, it was my opinion they were praying for what was best for the goals of the church, not me. I believe I was just a pawn. As a result, the battle continued. The Elder's advice not only remained the same but had a renewed fervour.

Diary October 9, 1982: Today the Elder's called us to another meeting. John opened by reading scripture from Jeremiah, Psalms and Proverbs. He said, " In Psalm 37 it says that we must turn to the Lord, do good and we must commit our ways to Him. Then in 1 Corinthians 10:22 it says that although all things are lawful, not all things are profitable. I want and I know you want to do the things that will be the most profitable in light of our work here on earth and in light of eternity"

Ron added, " I know what you two are experiencing but it says in Jeremiah 17:1-8 that the heart is deceitful above all else. You may have all the best intentions in the world but if the heart is what you are following, you are deceived. I know from past experience that it is difficult to see a situation clearly when you are emotionally involved. What is best for your lives and for all of us for that matter, is that both of you need to be spending more of your time meditating on the Word and on things that are pure."

"It says in Proverbs 16:1-3 and 19:20-21, that if you commit your ways to the Lord, your thoughts will be established, and that many are the plans in a man's heart but it is the counsel of the Lord that will stand. Our counsel to you is that you must do whatever is necessary to secure undistracted devotion to God. You will want to be able to handle the Word of Truth accurately so you will be able to discipline others and bear fruit in your life", explained John.

143

Ron turned to Grant and said, "You need to be doing similar things and learn to be closer to your brothers. Learning to live with others, before marriage, is an important step."

"Don't despair", said John. "If it is God's will for you to be together, it will happen no matter what. In the meantime, there is nothing at all that indicates to us that this relationship is God's will. According to 1Corinthians 13, you must be patient, love is patient and does not seek its own interests. In 2 Timothy 2:22, it also says to flee from youthful lusts. If you really love God, you will want to do everything for Him and His glory. That means giving up your own desires for the sake of the Gospel. This relationship is hindering both of you from walking effectively for the Gospel."

When Grant had left the room, Ron took me aside and said, "You can tell Grant that if his feelings for you change, that is OK and he is forgiven and that I forgive him. Let him know that it is alright. I know you aren't happy about this right now. In Hebrews 12:11 it says that discipline for the moment is sorrowful but afterwards it yields the peaceful fruit of righteousness. You have to learn to accept discipline."

A few days later I met with Ron alone to tell him what God had shown me and that I believed Grant was the future husband God picked for me. Ron listened and I was surprised when he did not change his position. On top of that, Ron told me that the Elders were very disturbed by Grant's behaviour. I was told that Grant went on his vacation road trip with his brother to the United States, without permission. In fact the Elders told him not to go and he went anyway. Ron said they felt that Grant needed to grow more in his faith before thinking about marriage. Ron concluded by telling me that the trip Grant took, only confirmed to himself and the other Elders, that Grant was not in control of his rebellious nature.

I stayed silent after Ron finished. I had to keep my lips sealed tight because I wanted to scream. Did they not know I had been doing everything they had been telling me to do and more? I did not need to be told to seek God. I had not been doing what the Elder's asked in relation to strengthening my faith because I was told to. Surely they should know by now, I had been sincerely seeking God all along. In fact long before coming to UBS. It was my pilgrimage to know God that brought me to UBS in the first place.

Did they not know that I had committed my life to God and had been working day and night on furthering the Gospel for this church? Other than my job, that is all I did. I had been giving this matter with Grant, over to God through prayer, again and again. I had been doing all the things they had been telling me I needed to do, for a couple of years now. I was not a child and I was a mature person who knew her own mind and heart. I did pray and I knew God's voice and did everything to follow it and do what I knew was right. Why could these Godly men, as I was told by everyone that they were, not see that? The gap between the attitude of the Elder's and my reality was incredulous. The only conclusion I could find, to reconcile these two worlds, was the disturbing realization that the Elder's were not interested in God's will, just my obedience and submission to their authority.

Grant and I met up in the cafeteria, during our lunch break, in November 1982. We had not been spending a lot of time together but on occasion we would meet. The wrath of the Elder's was something we wanted to avoid. We were still mostly writing letters to one another. We spoke sometimes at meetings within the BDG but we had tried to keep our talks casual and infrequent, so we could be less conspicuous. This lunch hour, Grant was not his usual confident self. He seemed nervous.

Grant started the conversation with what sounded like the reciting of a speech and he was stumbling and stammering over the words. Finally he abandoned whatever it was he was struggling with and blurted out that he cared for me and wanted to be able to do that for a long time to come. Eventually he said he wanted to spend the rest of his life with me. For clarification, I asked if he was talking about marriage or wanted us to just live together. He said wanted to marry me. He wanted to know if I would say yes. I paused, then smiled and said yes. Other lunch goers at the tables around us had been listening to the entire awkward conversation. As I looked up, I realized the public nature of our conversation. Everyone in earshot had stopped talking and were all looking at us and smiling. How wonderful it was to see these faces of people who were sincerely happy for us, even if they were strangers. I had hoped our Christian family members would smile upon us too.

Grant and I went to Ron right away to tell him about our decision. Ron did not react the way I had expected. He looked resigned to the fact that this was going to happen no matter what they said. I was pleasantly shocked when Ron said he was happy for us. He said we had his blessing but he would have to talk to the other two Elders about this. Until the other Elders agreed we understood that this would not be official. I knew that this was God's will for us and could not foresee any problems so I told my roommates the news and that we had Ron's blessings. This was a happy day and I felt so relieved that I could finally see a peaceful end to all this fighting about my private life.

Based on my news and my tentative support, my roommates had a change of heart. They even baked a cake for me to celebrate. We also told Jason and his wife but they were more guarded in their reactions. They did however say they were happy for us as well. Grant and I were confident that all the Elders would now realize that this was meant to be. Plus we had Ron's blessing and had tried our best to adhere to all their rules. It was a week later that we received the news that we had to meet with all three Elders again. The meeting was set to be in the Arts Building this time. Grant and I were hopeful for the first time in a long time.

I was more nervous than usual however. These meetings with the Elders were emotionally brutal. I felt sick to my stomach, so I went up to the prayer room on the top floor of the Student Union Building to pray in the hour before the meeting. I was reading from my *New Testament* when two Muslim women arrived for their prayers. Because their prayers were said out loud, I was distracted and went to another room to review the notes I had made in preparation for the meeting. I had a list of pros and cons to marrying Grant. I had written *Bible* verses that Grant and I felt were consistent with our good intentions. It was important that the Elders knew that we were coming at this from a solid foundation and that this was not just some youthful lust as they continually tried to suggest.

When the Elders arrived in the designated classroom, they sat at a large table at the front of the room like a panel of judges. Grant and I sat apart from one another in the desks facing the Elders near the middle of the room. I wanted some distance. Jeff told us how Ron had conveyed to him our belief that marriage was God's will for us. Jeff and Brian said that they had searched their hearts, considered all the facts again very carefully and then prayed about this some more. The three Elders were now in agreement that we had some serious growing up to do in our Christianity and that marriage would have to wait. We were still not allowed to see each other and the initial edict would stand as is. Our most egregious failure and shortcoming was the inability to accept the counsel of the Elders and become more obedient. They said God showed them that our relationship was not God's, will at least at this time.

I was now more convinced than ever that they had made some sort of mistake. After all, I told them what God had shown me and what I knew was true. I attempted to review my list of pros and cons so that they could see that we had given this a lot of careful thought and consideration. I tried to recite the list of *Bible* verses to strengthen what we believed was our intent for good. However, nobody was listening. Jeff just continued on the same train of thought, adding that there were too many areas of our lives that needed improvement before we could get married. I was told I needed to become more assertive and more aggressive in standing up for myself. It was obvious they had made some wrong assumptions about me as a woman of small stature with a quiet voice. In any case, isn't this exactly what I was doing, standing up, was I not?

Jeff told Grant that he needed to learn how to be closer to the brothers and build up those relationships first. He said we both needed to learn to submit to the Elders, that we were both being rebellious and needed to repent. Our inability to submit to him, Ron and Brian was a clear indication of our wrong attitudes, our pride and our rebellion before God. Jeff added that a relationship fostered in this environment could never be from God. Jeff said that as far as he and the other Elders were concerned, we were not engaged to be married and we were forbidden to see or talk to one another as we had been told before.

I was horrified. Grant and I had decided to become engaged and this was our decision, was it not? I loved this church and my friends and had committed myself to this work. There was nowhere else to go where the church was

148

as committed, zealous and radical as this one. UBS was fulfilling what God wanted in a way that was more patterned after the scriptures, than any other church I knew. I wanted to be a part of that. Could Grant and I try harder and wait for the Elders to change their minds? Was that possible and would they ever consent? Now I was confused. Were we still engaged or not? This was not about God's will as I suspected. This was about the Elders' need for us to submit to them and break us. Grant remained silent the entire time except for he occasional groan of disapproval and disbelief.

Ron had completely turned his back on us after giving his blessing. Everyone else who also said they supported us followed suit. Kari, Beth and Donna always followed what the Elders said. They never dared to question them like we had. Kari always opposed our engagement and now, so did Beth and Donna, again. Jason and his wife also sided with the Elders and withdrew their support for us. The only support we had left was Eileen and Stuart, our non-UBS friends. They had gotten to know Grant through me. Once they heard about the engagement and the Elder's admonishment, they became more concerned for us. They did not judge us and always said they were there for us if we ever needed them.

Grant and I spent a long time discussing and processing what happened. Nothing between us had changed and nothing with the Elders had changed. We decided that the Elders could not cancel our engagement, that was our choice. I was going home for Christmas. We planned for Grant to come with me, so he could meet my parents. But spies were everywhere and before we could finalize the plans, the Elders intervened and forbade him from going. In the recesses of my mind, I was still hoping that if we could show them we could follow their counsel, perhaps they would give us their blessing, some day. I am not sure Grant had that same hope. Grant complied with their wishes. I suspected the only reason he did was to please me and protect me from them.

CHAPTER FOURTEEN

When I returned from my Christmas travels, Jason, the brother responsible for Grant, pulled me aside at a meeting and said, "I am worried about you being with Grant. You can be easily talked into things by him. Grant is very persuasive and I am concerned about where this could lead. You need to step back and test your relationship with him. You need to allow God to take His course in Grant's life whether it be good or bad. As his older brother I want to protect him. You however, allow Grant to get away with being dishonest by allowing him to be only partially open when communicating therefore leading him into slander, rebellion and disobedience. You need to stick to your convictions and the counsel you have been given and discipline Grant by taking the proper action. You are going to have to call me or Ron if Grant won't listen to you and disobeys the counsel."

"I am sorry Jason but you are wrong about Grant. I don't agree with your advice. He is not dishonest and as far as disobedience goes, I don't think...", I said as I was interrupted from continuing.

"Just listen to what I am telling you", Jason cut in. "We

care about you and Grant. I want you to stay in close contact with myself, Beth or the Elders. You must learn to stick to your guns and be stronger. You must be righteous and not allow unrighteousness but at the same time encourage Grant. Don't correct him all the time. Be very careful to watch the area related to finances, being able to put problems aside until the appropriate time, dishonesty and slander. Don't let him play the devil's advocate and turn you against the others, especially the Elders. If Grant has a problem, ask him if he has taken his problem to the Lord first, then the Elders. If he hasn't directed him that way immediately. If he won't do that, phone me and then walk away from him."

When you care about someone, it hurts to hear people saying bad things about them. I felt more hurt about what Jason said about Grant even though he was extremely disrespectful of me. He did not know me and he did not know Grant. Grant and I had become close and shared a lot about our lives and our feelings with each other in our letters. I knew him better than the others and because everyone was so quick to judge him, he was reluctant to open up to other people. I can see why. Plus he knew me better than even my roommates.

I had been friends with my roommates for a long time now but the sharing was mostly one sided. They never gave me the opportunity to share who I was with them. I listened to them, learned from them and because they saw me as younger in Christ, they never sought out my advice or were interested in my wealth of experience. Only Donna, Grant and I were in the position to really get to know one another. So just as I felt they had underestimated Donna, they had no idea of who Grant was. They also had no idea who I was. The stereotype of a weak little girl with no mind of her own, that Jason and others had obviously associated with me, was very wrong.

I was starting to get angry with Jason's negative diatribe about Grant. I said "But Jason, it is not that simple. I tried to do what the Elders said but I just don't feel right about it. I don't think Grant is what you think he is. You are wrong about him and you are wrong about me."

Jason cut me off again and said with a mounting sense of urgency, "I know this must be painful for you but I can see things in Grant that you don't see. No matter how painful it is, you just can't cushion his fall or interfere with what the Lord is doing in his life by comforting him. You must let him take his problems to the Lord. The Lord tests us and all the things that are put in our lives are for us to learn and become more refined. Don't talk to Grant about things you shouldn't discuss like marriage,"

Jason went on to talk about how it would not be best for Grant to be married right now. He indicated that because I was the more mature Christian, it was up to me to take control of the situation and do what is best for Grant. Jason assured me that loyalty to the Elders was far more important than my allegiance to Grant because they, the Elders, had my best interests in mind. He insinuated that Grant did not. He then again begged me to report to the Elders or to him, right away, if Grant did not back off as I requested.

Beth and I shared a big bedroom. Before falling asleep that night Beth said to me, "If you and Grant want your characters to change so you will be ready for marriage, you had better start following the Elders advice. Grant is younger and he depends on you. You are preventing him from going to other people for advice as he should be doing. You are going to have to do something to stop this. You are going to have to start by pointing out to him his wrong attitude towards authority and his relationship with Jason. If his heart's attitude is wrong, so is his relationship to God. Pride can be a large factor in why this counsel is not taken properly. Being entangled in worldly affairs affects our Christian witness. It is God's will for Grant to be here but remember God's will is not based on feelings. Grant has not been able to make friends in the church because of you."

I was being hammered by everyone and just wanted to be left alone. I was also becoming more confused because this advice was not just coming from the higher ups in the church but from those I respected and considered to be my closest friends. I know both Grant and I had been shown that we were meant to be together but virtually the whole world was trying to convince us that this was a lie. Either I was terribly deceived or they were wrong. These were sincere people who loved God and prayed about things like this. Actually they prayed specifically about us. These people were the authorities on Christianity, not me.

Grant just felt that there was no real love in this church and that the Elders just didn't understand us. He felt the Elders did not understand what we were telling them. They were not listening to us. Grant did not agree with the counsel at all. He did not agree with a lot of things the Elders were teaching nor did he agree with some of the things the Elders were saying and doing. For example setting ourselves apart from non-believers. Grant felt this was wrong. I too had been questioning that. I was being pulled apart from all sides and did not know what to do. I was becoming even more weary and stressed.

I started having nightmares where I would be with Grant talking to him and then he would turn into the red fellow with the pitchfork. I also dreamed that I turned into a demon and was an enemy of God, while being powerless to change myself or choose sides. In my dreams I believed that I was becoming aligned to Satan but could not stop it. I could not sleep. I was waking up with anxiety attacks because I felt like I could not breathe. The stress I was experiencing started to become noticeable to those who knew me and I could no longer hide it.

The only person that voiced concern was Eileen. Her brother in law was a Christian counsellor who was working in the field of education for the United Church. Eileen wanted me to talk to him but I was not thrilled about talking to someone outside of UBS. We were taught that the other churches were lukewarm and not doing God's will. We were taught to guard ourselves against these Christians who UBS had taught us, had wandered away from the truth. I was worried that I was being tricked by the devil to see this man. However, I trusted Eileen who had consistently shown that she cared about me and who had shown herself to be, in my opinion, a very wise and Godly woman.

I thought about it for a couple of weeks and my anxiety was not getting any better. I knew I needed someone who would take the time to listen to what I had to say, without passing judgment. Up until this point, nobody in UBS had heard a single word I had said. I desperately needed to talk to someone outside my immediate circle, so I agreed to see Robert. Once I told Eileen of my decision, she wasted no time in making the arrangements and picking me up to visit her family in the next town. Normally I would be apprehensive about such a trip but I had lost my fight, I was feeling weak and resigned. I was alone. I needed help and knew it. I was willing to take whatever caring and support I could find. My family could not help. The only people who could help me were other Christians who understood the details and subtleties of the theology that had infiltrated the life I was now leading.

Robert, his wife and family lived on the same property as Eileen's mom. She lived in a second smaller building behind the main house. While we waited for Robert to come and get me, I got acquainted with Eileen's mother.

Together we watched TV and chatted over tea. Eileen and her mom did most of the talking while I listened. The women were exchanging views on a variety of psychological and spiritual subjects.

I was interested in what they had to say about an experiment they had both read about. It was set up with three people. One person was placed inside a soundproof box and was asked some questions by a second person outside the box. If the answer to the question was incorrect, this second person was instructed by a third person, to administer a dosage of electric shock. The third member was the person in charge and was responsible for the amounts of electricity to be administered. With each wrong answer, the magnitude of shock was increased until a lethal dosage was reached. The experiment was designed to see what the second person would do when ordered to give a dose and who would kill the person in the box.

The lethal dose did not actually exist. It was concluded after testing a wide range of people from many areas of society were tested, that people who respected authority were among those most likely to kill another person. The most dangerous people were the quiet, law abiding, do-good folks, who would never harm anyone under normal circumstances. These were the folks who were reluctant to question authority. They believed that if someone else in authority was responsible and that someone else was accountable, then it was OK, they would be just doing their job.

The retelling of this story by Eileen and her mother intrigued me. It kindled the flicker of a light bulb moment for me. I bookmarked this story in my mind and knew it was significant for me to remember and think about this. I wondered what kind of person I was? Before I was able to consider this in any depth, Robert came for me. He was small in stature, had a beard and was soft spoken. We were

156

introduced and then he invited me to follow him across the yard, to his office. He told me a bit about himself and his clinical practice. Then he asked me to tell him what was happening to me. He just listened and never interrupted as I went on and on. Finally he asked me to repeat something I had said. I repeated to him that I was confused because on one hand I really wanted to marry Grant but on the other hand I also wanted to be obedient to the Elder's counsel and do what was best.

Robert then made a simple observation. He said that when I talked about being obedient to the Elder's counsel, I looked away to the side, my eyes became blank and I became distant, detached and my facial expression was one of sadness. When I said I wanted to marry Grant, my eyes were focused toward him, there was light, a sparkle in my eyes, I was engaged in the conversation, clear, alert and present. Robert told me that this was the difference between death and life in me. The sadness was death and the light was life. Then he went on to describe how the life and death that Jesus spoke about was not necessarily the biological aspect we usually associate with these words. I felt I was beginning to understand what was happening. For the first time in a long time, I felt the fog starting to dissipate.

Robert spoke about how the spirit of oppression and the spirit of passivity go hand in hand. That this had some bearing on my not being able to stand on my own and make decisions. He gave examples of how Jesus encountered opposition as well and he said that I could not let other people's lack of peace about something affect me. The Lord alone is my teacher and I must stand before God on my own. I was the person that needed to judge what was best for me. My willingness to settle for peace rather than rock the boat, would have far reaching consequences in my life. My dependence on my church and the fear of leaving UBS, would also have far reaching consequences.

He added that peace in the world's terms is different from true peace. True peace is not quietness and lack of disturbance but can only come when all things are reconciled.

I told Robert about the terrible guilt I felt for not obeying the Elders. Robert said that there are two types of guilt that Peter talks about in the *New Testament*. Guilt that produces sorrow and and leads to repentance, is the work of God. Guilt that comes from the world, produces death by binding and immobilizing a person. Robert told me to be free and learn about freedom but don't disregard the Elder's advice. Learn when to stand, when to speak and when to fight. He said freedom would be scary because we all prefer to remain within the comfort of our learned behaviours. He gave me the verses in Galatians 5:1, 4:9 and Romans 8:15 as references to review.

Robert also said that burdens can sometimes be self inflicted and so can guilt. He said that the moment I started to ask myself if God was really the kind of being that the Elders described, or wonder if God was really punishing me for my disobedience, then red lights should have been flashing. When I started to doubt my understanding of the character of God and who God was, I should have seen this as a danger signal. Jesus never stopped Peter from denying Him and He did not punish Peter for doing so. Jesus restored Peter without question. Should I pay a penalty for not doing God's will? I realized then that even if I was not doing God's will, He would not have punished me as the Elders insinuated. The Elder's actions towards me led me to believe I was being punished by God because I was being punished by them. I now knew that there was something terribly wrong with what was happening to me.

I was starting to realize how much of a hold UBS had on me and that that was not good. I could see the influence they had but I did not yet understand enough to explain it. I was, however, now better able to think about my situation in a different light. I felt heard, validated and felt I had more confidence in my own gut feel and my relationship with Christ. I knew that I could put more faith in myself and look at life around me from my own perspective. I knew that somehow, I needed to put away the goggles of religious teaching through which I had been taught to view the world. It was time for me to find that person I had lost, fight for regency over my own life and regain my autonomy.

CHAPTER FIFTEEN

Those moments of clarity that came to me when visiting with Eileen's family, would be my salvation. However, nothing was going to be simple or easy. I was afraid of the implications of what I had realized. I found it difficult to focus on what I had learned and my mind wandered back and forth from its new unfamiliar territory to the old comfortable world according to UBS. On one hand I was convinced the church and the Elders were wrong about me. On the other hand I had trouble believing that a group of people I saw as sincerely devoted to God, could be so wrong. I wondered who I should be listening to because the wisdom of God is far greater than the wisdom of men. UBS was adamant that they followed the Word of God. I found myself thinking about what Robert said and the confidence I felt in myself afterwards. Then a few minutes later, I would be afraid that Robert was being manipulated by Satan to fool me. Grant and I later called this mental gymnastics "flipping".

To complicate matters I was still convinced somehow that UBS and the sister churches around the world were the best churches. I believed that UBS was God's church following God's will. I was terrified to leave the church because I would not be doing the best for God. It would mean that I settled for being a lazy Christian just going through the motions, instead of a zealous soldier for God. The Elders were wrong about Grant and I but they were right about other things. If they were right about my rebelliousness, I am not sure if that was such a bad thing. They also told me I had to learn to stand up for myself. Wasn't that what I was doing? The advice they gave was contradictory. I had lost faith in the Elders but not in the church.

I promised myself I would not tell anyone about my session with Robert. However I did end up telling Beth. She told me I had to be very careful and she warned me that it would be better that I not talk to Robert again. Beth said he may be a wolf in sheep's clothing and that she did not think I was mature enough to distinguish who was a sheep and who was a wolf. She said the only way to tell is by the fruit of the spirit in the person's life. The good fruit would be love, joy, peace and patience. I also needed to look for Christ-likeness in the person. She said she had known the Eiders for a long time and they were the most holy men she had ever met. She would not trust anyone else and neither should I. I told her that I did not see the Christ-like qualities in the Elders and that perhaps I just did not know them well enough. She said she knew and that I could trust her judgment.

As a result of my confession to Beth, the Elders wanted to see Grant and I yet again. By now, we had been spending more time together. We had chosen not to do what the Elders said but we did so infrequently and discreetly. Before we went to the meeting, Grant and I prayed together. We asked that the Elders, for once, would hear us and see our side of the matter. When Eileen heard about the meeting, she asked me to write down what I expected of the Elders this time. I documented what I expected as well as what I hoped would be accomplished.

In any case, no matter what happened, I was planning to remain steadfast to my decision to marry Grant.

Diary January 15, 1982 *My Wished-For Expectations: In a perfect world and in a world that is right, the Elders will listen carefully and non-judgmentally hear and understand what we tell them. They will learn about who we really are and see our dilemma. They will tell us what is best but ask us what we think we can do to strike a happy medium between what we feel God wants and the deficiencies they think they see. Perhaps seeing that the marriage is inevitable, they could rally support for us through the church and offer us marriage counselling. Even if they don't agree, they will respect us, our decision and support us no matter what. That is what I expect the Elders to do if they are following Christ's teachings about love. Hopefully they will see that love for us and acceptance is far more important.*

My Realistic Expectations: I expect that two of the three Elders will be surprised by my position. They will think Grant has talked me into this because they have assumed I am naive. They will make accusations about our lives not being what they should be and that our failings are a result of our not following their counsel to begin with. They will think of us as rebellious and sinful. They will give us some things to think about, ask us to reconsider our decision to get married and then get back to us. I expect that I won't be able to change their minds no matter how much I tell them about how I feel. Their decisions and judgments will have been made before we even open our mouths. I expect that they will talk about us leaving the church.

When we arrived at the meeting we were outnumbered five to two. The three Elders were there plus Jason and Beth. They opened the meeting by reading some verses from scripture.

*1 Peter 5:15, Hebrews 11:12, Titus 1:5 and 1 Timothy
5:13: Therefore I exhort the elders among you, as your
fellow elder and witness of the sufferings of Christ and
partaker also of the glory that is to be revealed, Shepherd
the flock of God among you, not under compulsion but
voluntarily, according to the will of God, and not for
sordid gain, but with eagerness, nor yet as lording it over
those allotted to your charge, but proving to be examples
to the flock. And when the chief Shepherd appears, you
will receive the unfading crown of glory. You young men
likewise be subject to your elders, and all of you, clothe
yourselves with humility towards one another, for God is
opposed to the proud but gives grace to the humble....Do
not receive an accusation against an elder except on the
basis of two or three witnesses. Those who continue in sin,
rebuke in the presence of all so that the rest also may be
fearful of sinning...*

The Elders also read many verses from Acts and
instructed us on the role of elders in the church and how
they should be respected and treated. At the end of the
lecture, they again told us not to see each other any more.
Grant was really upset, as was I. We never even had the
chance to speak let alone be heard. Grant motioned for me
to leave the room with him about half way through. He
was so angry that he wanted to just walk away but he
would not leave without me. I couldn't go. I was still
clinging to my wishes, expectations and the now fading
dream that it would work out, if we were just patient. I was
devastated and told Beth on the way home in the car, that if
the Elders did not back off and leave us alone, we would
both leave the church. I did not know if I would or even if I
could, but I felt strongly that this was where we had landed
on the matter.

I wanted to leave the church so I could be with Grant
and end the continuous harassment and interference into

the most personal aspects of my life. The whole thing was ludicrous and intolerable. We had been tremendously hurt by the false accusations, blatant lack of respect and guilt laden humiliation and coercion. But while my instincts told me to leave, fear and logic worked against that, telling me not to. Everyone who knew these Elders said they were Godly men and those that knew them had a lot of respect for them. They had been devoted to this cause for a long time. I could never be as devoted as I am told they are. Who was I to question them?

If it wasn't for this church, I would probably slip back into sinful ways. My gut told me that God would be with me wherever I went but the other UBSers told me I was arrogant for thinking such a thing. Was I just blinded by pride? Would I be leaving God and His chosen path, if I left the church? Maybe the Lord's discipline was too much for me and I was not faithful or dedicated enough to accept it. I frequently flipped back and forth from my comfortable UBS mindset and my newly emerging instinctive, questioning, free, light filled mindset. In the end I knew, this was my life and I was accountable for me.

I hoped I could marry Grant and stay in the church. That was my hope and my plan. I tried to carry on with my life as best I could and maintain some semblance of normality. I continued on with my work at the university and in the church, attending meetings, events, spending time with my roommates, my new friend Eileen and with Grant. Grant and I were very secretive about our time together, very low key with the predominance of our communication through letter writing. I was still not totally sure how to move forward and was apprehensive as to how this would turn out. I was not responsible for the discomfort of others. My choices felt good, based in love and I was at peace knowing I was doing the right thing. That was the best I could do.

I thought if I just ignored the Elders, they would eventually come to accept me as I was. Maybe if I laid low and was discreet, they would just leave me alone. That was like saying, if I close my eyes, nobody will see me. Our letter writing depended also on the discretion of the letter handlers. The fellow church members chosen were considered trustworthy but that was not the case. Both my roommates and Grant's were keeping close tabs on everything we did and reported all the details back to the Elders. Grant also became a little too exuberant and sent two dozen long white and red stemmed roses to my apartment. Then one night Grant and I drove around enjoying the snow and laughing until early morning. We had lost track of time.

I knew that staying out all night was not going to go over well with my roommates. The flowers had already caused some trouble as it was. We knew we had already stayed out too long, too many hours ago. There was no use going home now. Instead we stopped at Tim Horton's for breakfast. Even then, I felt ridiculous sneaking into the apartment at six am. I didn't even bother to offer any explanations to anyone because if I had told them that we had a delightful and innocent time talking and laughing, they would never believe me. Kari and Beth had a private conference in Kari's room after I arrived home. I suspect they were talking about and praying for me. I felt bad that I had caused them so much grief.

A week later I arrived home from grocery shopping with Kari and Beth, to find Ron waiting for us outside the apartment building. Ron told me he wanted to meet with me last week and I refused, telling him that going forward, Grant and I would only meet with them if we were together. Grant and I promised each other we would never allow ourselves to be alone with an Elder again. This time I was trapped and soon realized that my roommates had instigated this. I believed they felt I was much weaker than

166

Grant and were singling me out to try and break me. Eileen had coached me about what to do if I should find myself in another meeting with the Elders, so I had mentally prepared myself and had a plan.

Just as Ron started to pray and open the meeting, the phone rang. Beth answered it and I could tell it was Eileen looking for me. Beth told her I could not talk right now and hung up. I found out later that Beth had actually pulled the plug out of the wall to prevent Eileen from calling back. After the prayer Ron complained about my rebellious and self-willed nature while reading Titus 1:6-7. He again reminded me that I was to be in subjection to my Elders and submit to them while quoting 1 *Corinthians* 16:16 and Hebrews 13:17. Ron then described what love was according to 1*Corinthians* 13. He said love does not seek its own and that I had a serious problem with a lack of love because I was seeking a relationship with Grant, that was more important to me, than my relationship to my roommates and the church.

He added that, he who separates himself, seeks his own desire; that I shouldn't do anything from selfishness and that I shouldn't quarrel against all sound wisdom (Proverbs 18:1, Philippians 2:3). Ron said my heart was deceived and I was way off track from the truth. Then he went on to read more from the *Bible*.

Matthew 18: 15-17: ...and if your brother sins, go and reprove him in private. If he listens to you, you have won your brother. But if he does not listen to you, take one or two more with you, so that by the mouth of two or three witnesses every fact may be confirmed. And if he refused to listen to them, tell it to the church, and if he refuses to listen to even the church, let him be to you as a Gentile and a tax gatherer.

Ron told me again that I had three areas of sin in my

life: rebelliousness, selfishness and lack of love. He said Satan was playing a game with my life and was trying to destroy me. He told me to ask God how true these things were (as if I hadn't been asking that very thing, daily for months). He said I had a hard heart and must repent. Then he began crying and pleading with me to repent. I mentally and emotionally removed myself from the emotion. I stayed calm, evaluated the situation and moved to the role of the observer. This helped cushion the very personal attacks against me and helped me to remain objective.

In the middle of Ron's continued pleading, I stood up and walked out of the room to get one of my journals. I returned with the book open and a pen in hand and began to write down every word that was being said, as Eileen had instructed me to do. Ron was somewhat startled because I just calmly walked out while he was crying and emotional. This caused him to lose some of his confidence and he became nervous. I then looked directly at him and told him that I wanted to make sure that I did not miss a single word.

As I observed the entire deluge, I remember likening it to what I imagined was the twilight zone, like in those TV movies. OK, maybe I was not the most loving person in the world. I had confessed that and that was something I could have done better. However, that was between God and myself. God had forgiven me and was working on it. I was not guilty and they were trying to convince me I was. As far as being selfish, I had been working on the goals of the church, committing my life to working for the church day and night for years. I had been doing what everyone else wanted me to do, my roommates and even trying to accommodate the Elder's requests. I had been working yet did not own anything of significance. Having a special relationship with someone I cared about, that was not selfish, it was natural and beautiful. Was I rebellious, yes I was but it was not in my nature to be like that. I loathe confrontation. The ridiculous rules that were impossible to follow gave me no choice but to rebel. The Elders created this rebellion.

I sat on the floor making my notes and evaluating these accusations. I remained calm and weighed what was being said. Then I came back to the present moment and allowed myself to feel the indignance of it all and the hurt. I felt outrage for the injustice and the bullying, that this meeting and the other meetings not only allowed but instigated against me, the younger less experienced, the one they were supposed to care for, not abuse. I started to cry, in sorrow for how I had been misunderstood and mistreated by everyone I was close to. I was not weeping in repentance but in disbelief and anger. I looked around at each person in the room. Each had a satisfied and relieved look on their face because they thought they had won and had broken my will. However, just to be clear that this was not what they thought, I proclaimed that, "this is not from God, this meeting is not the work of God."

Disappointed, Ron immediately pronounced his conclusion, that I was hard of heart. He quoted *Matthew* 3:5 and 18:17 saying that the fruit of my repentance and the thing that would prove my repentance was that I wouldn't see or speak to Grant ever again. He said excommunication was less severe than allowing sin in the church. He read 1 *Corinthians* 5:37 and proclaimed that it was not God's will for Grant and I to have a relationship at all and that partnership did not produce the fruit of the spirit. He said that we would have the worst marriage in the world and that we would tear each other apart.

Kari then read from *Hebrews*12 saying that all discipline is painful for the moment. She said that God was very gracious but if we (Grant and I) continued to rebel, God would take all those who were close to us away. Beth then read *Hebrews* 5:13-14 about discerning good and evil.

169

She said the Word indicated that Grant and I are rebellious, that the Biblical description of a rebellious person matched Grant and I. Ron repeated that the Elders are responsible before God for our souls. Then he again quoted *Hebrews* 13:17 that says to obey your leaders and submit to them for they watch over your soul.

I continued to sit cross legged on the centre of the carpet on the living room floor. Ron was sitting on the couch facing me. Kari and Beth were sitting in the armchairs beside me to the left and the right. I refused to admit that I was in sin, beg for their forgiveness and promise to never see Grant again. This is what they wanted me to do but it was just not true and it was not right. I remained on the floor with my head bowed. I refused to further answer or respond and remained silent. I remained steadfast to my convictions that I was innocent of the charges against me. I moved away from being present in the moment to becoming the observer again, to calm my nerves, deaden the pain, analyze and strategize. Finally Ron motioned to everyone that there was nothing more that they could do and he got up and walked out.

While I was still sitting on the living room floor, Kari and Beth got up and went about getting supper ready as if nothing had happened. Donna came into the room and saw me and looked at Kari and Beth with a questioning expression. Then the three of them went into one of the bedrooms and closed the door to discuss and update Donna, I presumed. Nothing was said when they came back to the kitchen. I just stood in one corner of the room looking down with my hands in my pockets. I was frozen in place in disbelief and shock watching Beth with her back to me, moving from the cupboard to the table with plates and dishes, then from the stove to the fridge and back again. My mind was screaming. I needed to tell someone what happened. I needed to find Eileen and Grant.

I felt myself change into survival mode and analyze my options and the repercussions. I needed to get help with the least amount of commotion and awareness from the church. I was not sure what my next step would be or what I could say without losing my home in the process. To measure the temperature of the water, I broke the silence and said to Beth, "What would happen now if I went to see Grant?"

Beth responded coldly, "If you go and see Grant now, after what was said here, you would be going directly against Ron's instructions for your need to show repentance. There would be no choice but for you to immediately leave our household. You will be excommunicated and I will not be able to speak to you or have anything to do with you, ever again."

"How soon would I have to leave?", I queried, not sure I heard correctly the first time.

"Immediately, if you go and see Grant", Beth repeated, loud and clear so that there would be no misunderstanding.

With that obtuse clarification, I got my coat and walked out of the apartment without speaking. For a long time I drove around in shock. I passed by the university and somehow met up with Grant. He was wandering around campus I believe, in shock like I was. He had a story to tell that was similar to mine. I didn't even remember getting into the car and my head was spinning. These terrible deeds were done to me by the church I believed in and by my dearest, closest confidantes. I was about to lose my home, my security and all the things that were most important in my life, just because I wanted to marry the person I was in love with. This was crazy scary.

I had no intention of cutting off my relationship to

171

Grant. I knew what both my heart and God had shown me. I was shaken and afraid. I was having a hard time coming to terms with how my best friends had turned on me. A flood of doubt kept washing over me, threatening to leave me floating and drowned in a sea of accusations. Will my rebellion affect my relationship to God? Was I really loveless and selfish and just blind to my own desires to put myself above everyone else? Was I fooling myself and was I in sin so deep that I just couldn't see it? Was I going to hell for this?

The people that knew me best and who I loved were turning their backs on me, saying I was a terrible sinful monster. They better than anyone should have known that I loved Christ. They even supported me and had a celebration for my engagement, just a short while ago. Where did that go and how was it so quickly changed and extinguished. It was like the Elders had absolute control of everyone. So much so that they could switch people on or off like a light switch. I knew excommunication would be inevitable. I knew that I would give up everything to be with Grant but I could not accept why I had to make such a painful choice. As I floated in the ocean of uncertainty and fear, I clung to the knowledge that I loved Grant and we were meant to be.

As Grant and I sat in my car talking, we both knew we could not go back to our homes. We had nobody to turn to except Eileen and Stuart who repeatedly told us they were there if we ever needed them, any time of the day or night. Now we needed that refuge and went directly to their house but nobody was home. We went around to the patio doors in the back and left a little HELP sign on the glass. When they did return, we found out that they were out looking for us. Eileen became very concerned when Beth pulled the plug on the phone. She knew something was wrong when she repeatedly called back and got nothing. She wanted to jump in the car and come over to rescue me but was afraid of overreacting. Her emotional signals and insightfulness, however, were accurate.

Eileen and Stuart stayed up into the wee hours of the morning, listening to each of us recount our stories. They did not want us to make any decisions under duress, given the pending impact on our lives and our faith. Grant was not swimming in indecision like I was. Church members had tried to turn me away from Eileen in past months by saying she could not join UBS because she was not a dedicated enough Christian to make the cut. UBS even went as far as to dig into her past to try and discredit her with negative information. Perhaps I couldn't even trust her? I was feeling so many different things at the same time and I was flipping, again, between the programmed UBS self and the reemerging real me.

Maybe God wanted me to leave UBS but that I could not see the good in that just yet? However, although I was terrified to leave UBS, I knew that I could not go back in the same capacity. The fear, self-doubt, overwhelming guilt and cruel words of those I respected were constant forces tearing away at me. Instead I clung to my faith in Christ and His forgiveness. I cherished the knowledge that God loved me and would not abandon me. I also held tight to the conviction that Eileen was a true friend that really cared about me. We would have been homeless and may have had to go back to the church begging for a place to sleep. Stuart and Eileen wanted us to make an objective choice about our future. They offered for us to stay with them until we were better able to make sound decisions. These things, plus the understanding words and sage advice offered by both Robert and Eileen, were beacons in the stormy seas of my new adventure in freedom.

CHAPTER SIXTEEN

Robert was right, my fear of leaving UBS would have a lasting impact on my life. Deep down I knew I had to walk away from UBS. But all the counsel, what had been said and the hurt was holding me back. I could not reconcile what was in my heart with what was in my mind. I was so internally polarized that I was paralyzed. I couldn't leave Eileen's place until I had sorted this out. I had to make a decision. We were in Eileen and Stuart's bedroom that was set up with a couch and chair. It was the only private place to talk given they had five children. I laid on the bed while she relaxed on the coach and we talked for a long time. I don't know if it was an hour or a day.

Eileen had been encouraging me to write down everything that was happening to me in a journal and I had been doing that for months now. For the sake of my sanity I had to make a decision so I wrote a list of pros and cons about UBS. If I stayed with UBS, I knew I would be constantly under scrutiny. They would take all the joy of being engaged. If we finally did get approval from the Elders to be married, our new relationship of husband and wife would be strained from the added expectations of the roles dictated by the Elders. I needed freedom and acceptance and the chance to learn from more mature Christians.

I also needed a chance to learn and lean on God alone, stand before Him on my own and make my own choices, right or wrong. I decided that I would leave the apartment and my UBS household for a start. They would not have taken me back anyway unless I grovelled and begged for forgiveness for my sins. That was not going to happen. I also decided that the marriage was on and I would pick a date and start planning, Lord willing. I told Eileen what I had decided. She and I agreed that I would stay with their family until the wedding.

I was still in the bedroom when Grant arrived to see how I was doing. I did not know he had even left the house or how long I had been in the bedroom but there was a knock on the door and it was Grant. I soon knew Eileen had told him about my decision because he presented me with a lovely engagement ring. It looked like a flower with one larger diamond surrounded by smaller ones with seven in total. I put the ring on and vowed to myself that this ring was not only a sign of my commitment to Grant but also a promise to follow through on all the decisions I had just made.

Eileen supported me in whatever decision I made. She was careful not to influence my decisions but tried to set up conditions that would facilitate my free will. She never ever criticized UBS, the Elders or anyone in my church. She just gave me options so I could think without the pressure from UBS. She also counselled me in how to handle them in ways that would buffer any attacks. She reminded me that I had the right to be silent. That I did not have to tell anyone what I was doing and why. That it would be better if I did not say too much. She said that if I still went to the church events, she warned me not to say too much but observe what was happening around me. She suggested that I write down everything from reactions to my ring, the questions I was asked even facial expressions. If I was questioned about the ring, I should remain silent. Then she reinforced that no matter what anyone said, I was innocent. She made me look up and write down the definition of the word. I was God's child, I was blameless, not aware of evil and free from guilt.

I returned home to the apartment and told my roommates I was leaving. Kari reacted instantaneously. She was ferociously opposed to my decision and could not, before God, support me in any way. Beth on the other hand was disappointed and appeared sad. She maintained that she did not agree with me but that she would support me even if the Elders did not. Donna, who was feisty and had disagreements with the Elders before, also said she would support me. However I knew her support would fluctuate. Later on Beth convinced Kari she was wrong about me and Kari apologized. She said she would support me under the condition that I kept her informed about what was happening in my life and that I promised to pray with her about my marriage once a week. I was pleased to get Kari's belated support. I was not pleased with the conditions and was still profoundly sorrowful that it had come to this, my leaving. The new found goodwill from my roommates was too little too late.

That same evening that I told my roommates the news, I received a phone call from Ron encouraging me to stay at the apartment with Kari and Beth. He said, "Beth has told me about your plan to leave the household and she is very torn apart about the thought that you would leave. I think the move is too rash. I am sure that we can reason this thing out and come to some compromises to keep everyone happy. Now that you and Grant are at peace about your decision to get married, you won't be seeing very much of one another. I don't see why there should be any problems with your goals to get married and the goals of the household."

I was very pleased that Ron had finally decided to listen to what Grant and I had been saying. He was ready to compromise. This was great. This is what I had been hoping for. I had wanted to marry Grant and I prayed that the Elders would realize that they had made a mistake. They should not have interfered in our decision the way they did, nor did they know God's will for us. With the surprise and new optimism and without having carefully considered the actual words being said, I said, "Yes Ron, I think we can work this out too". When I hung up the phone, I started to think about what Ron said. Then I realized what had happened.

I had been tricked into agreeing to something I had no intention of doing. Near the end of that warm, lovely and rational sounding plea, was a comment about how Grant and I would no longer need to see each other anymore. He said there was room for compromise. I agreed that yes, we could work this out. But I now wondered, "...not see each other anymore..." but why was that? I looked at my ring. I had no intention of discontinuing the time I was spending with Grant. What compromises and who would be doing the compromising? I was so surprised by Ron's turn-around and syrupy voice, that I wanted to believe that we could make things work. But work for whom and on what terms?

Ron had also tried to make me feel bad for what I was doing to Beth. Poor Beth and my crushed roommates. He tried to make me feel guilty and took advantage of my hope for a compromise. The only person that ever was expected to compromise, all along, was me. Ron certainly was not about to change. He tricked me and struck a low blow by appealing to the welfare of those I cared about. He tried to weaken me emotionally. For the first time I saw how the Elders and my roommates had been playing on my feelings, emotions and my fears all along. In the end Ron had not apologized, did not admit he was wrong and was singing the same tune as always. I was innocent and I had been violated. Shame on them.

The very next morning on January 26, 1982, I waited for everyone in my household to leave. Then I immediately went to see Eileen. We both took time off work and drove her station wagon to the apartment. I went in alone while Eileen watched the street in case anyone returned. I packed as quickly as I could and took whatever I could fit in my knapsack and bags. There was not much and I did not feel I had time to take the large stuff. The plan was to make one trip in and one trip out. I was safe for the moment because after the phone call last night, Ron and my roommates believed they had convinced me to stay.

However, I wholeheartedly believed that if anyone from the church saw me moving out, someone would definitely try to stop me. At the very least they would try and manipulate me and I was not sure anymore if I could handle it. Questions and fears about leaving were still there in my subconsciousness. Ron had already tricked me last evening. I was determined to escape as quickly as possible and whatever was missed, I would leave behind. I needed to get out fast and I was never going back to that place ever again.

With Eileen's help I had successfully left the UBS household. However I had not yet made the decision to leave the church. I saw there were errors in the way the Elders had behaved towards me. I felt the Elders were in danger of leading the whole church astray by using too much power and assuming authority over people's personal lives. I know I was overly influenced by the Elders and felt being out of the household would give breathing space to sort out my questions about the church. I was still naively hoping that the Elders would see the error of their ways, apologize and bless our upcoming marriage.

The day after I left Kari and Beth's place Grant left his household with Jason and others. I shared the twin's bedroom with Eileen and Stuart's two youngest and Grant moved into the basement. We were both still working at the university and we paid Stuart and Eileen a small fee for room and board. It was not much and they basically just took us in and treated us like part of their family. In this environment, I found myself regaining my old self. I had realized and saw glimpses of things within UBS that I described at the time as being evil. Although I had begun to think more for myself again, and question everything, I was not able to put my finger on what was wrong with the church. Plus, I was still afraid that I would lose my faith and my dedication, if I left UBS. That underlying fear was keeping me there and preventing me from leaving.

As soon as Grant too moved out of his household, the Elders sent a message that they wanted to see us again together. They wanted another meeting with us. They said they had re-evaluated the jurisdiction of their authority and they realized that they couldn't really tell us if and when we could get married. They explained that they had been under a lot of pressure from other members of the church who did not believe we should get married. Other couples had to follow the Elder's counsel. Many waited years for approval to get married. Plus there were many singles in the church who were older and more mature than us. They couldn't understand why two of the youngest and newest members of the church were getting married before them.

Ron said, "I am sorry if we lead you into believing that disobeying counsel was sinful. Disobeying counsel is not sinful. It's just that every time I looked at you two all I could see was sin (there it was again, the backhanded slap in the face). Counsel is advice that that does not need to be taken but is only wise to do so (another slap). If you decide to get married, despite our advice, we will support you anyhow. You are like my children and I know it would be wrong to abandon them if they went astray (third slap). We want you to take our marriage lessons so we can know how you are doing and give you some guidelines to help you make the best of it (final slap, conditions plus a hook)."

The three Elders then said they had prayed again and still did not feel at peace about us getting married right now and their counsel still stood as before. Only now it was not a sin for us to disobey their counsel. They would support us, only if we took their marriage classes. At first we thought we had made tremendous progress towards a reconciliation. This was good news at first blush and we were happy until we replayed the words in our head. There were too many backhanded insults disguised as caring. In the end the Elders had not changed their position, their advice stood as it was. We asked the Elders to clarify what they told us, with the rest of the membership. They would not. We wanted everyone to know that we had not been excommunicated, that the Elders had backed off on this. They would not, this was a private matter.

The first UBS meeting I attended after leaving the household, was a Thursday evening class on other religions. One of the sisters asked me why I was nervous. I told her I was thinking of leaving the church. She told me that it must be scary going against the Elder's advice. Then she asked me, "How could you ever be arrogant enough to think that going against the Elder's advice would be God's will? How could you think God would be with you?" I told her that I wasn't prepared to discuss this with her. She replied, "What's wrong? Is it too inconvenient for you?"

A second sister joined us and began talking about how serious marriage was and how afraid she would be getting married even with the Elder's approval. She then said that when she turned twenty-three, she started to wonder if she would ever get married. I assumed she was projecting her concerns on me, thinking I was only getting married because I was worried I was getting older. Then both women shared experiences when they each had been filled with arrogance, pride and selfishness. Again I believe they were expecting me to share similar confessions and spark some sort of repentance in me. However I was not going to get sucked into that. I remained silent and this irritated them. They clearly had formed strongly negative opinions about me and they did not know me. Clearly the members of UBS were gossiping which I thought was considered a sin.

I soon found out that the majority of members of the church believed that Grant and I were in sin for disobeying the Elders and going ahead with our wedding. Members inside the church and even people not in the church were talking about how Grant and I were not disciplined enough or devoted enough in our Christian lives to follow the counsel of the Elders. They told each other they pitied us and were afraid for us because we could not do the right thing. There was even an emergency prayer meeting organized on our behalf to petition God to stop our wedding plans. Prayer meetings are a great way to share gossip hidden as a good deed.

Grant and I continued to be involved in UBS but we were finding it very painful. Everyone I spoke to believed I was in sin. They constantly challenged, questioned and disbelieved me. I was the subject of everyone's judgment and correction. They had imagined that Grant and I must be sinful in all areas of our lives since our marriage was not blessed by the Elders. There had to be some deep dark reason why the Elders withheld their consent. Many harboured jealousy and resentment towards us. Others were haughty and indignant, wondering, "Who the hell do they think they are?"

The Elders refused to correct the wrong thinking of the church members saying what they thought about us was of no importance. We tried to tell some people what the Elders said to correct them and then they accused us of slandering the Elders. As long as we did not have the blessing of the Elder's, we would not have the support of the rest of the congregation even though the Elders said they would support us. The rest of the congregation believed we were sinful for disobedience, slander, rebellion and therefore were unholy, ungodly people, vessels for the work of Satan. How did the Elders not know or care what was being said about us? The Elders enticed us to stay but the congregation was punishing us and we were being ostracized.

Gerry, the UBS Elder in training, was not only a professor at the university but worked in the same department as Eileen and I. We had been friends but I noticed when nobody else was around, he would turn his back and walk away from me if I tried to speak to him. This infuriated me and every time I confronted him about it, he would deny doing it. It seemed that the negative opinions of Grant and I had now spread from my church to my workplace. I was finally able to corner him one day and tell him how I saw that there was a serious problem with the way the Elders were running the church. I strongly pointed out to him how they had too much authority and that this was dangerous, especially if they were wrong about God's will. I told him the Elders were wrong in how they had treated Grant and I and behaviour like that could cause the entire church to be led astray and become "off track".

Gerry and I argued about this for a while with each of us using scripture to back up our positions. I won the discussion in that Gerry actually listened to me. He heard what I was talking about and understood what I was saying. He said he would talk to the Elders about these

183

concerns. I was ecstatic that someone understood the concerns I had and that perhaps the Elders would see their errors and make some necessary corrections in their teachings to address this.

However, even though Gerry saw the light, he flipped back to the UBS mindset when he saw the Elders. The next day he told me that he would never speak to me again because I was evil. He accused me of causing him to doubt the Elders and the church and I had made him waver in his faith. He said I had seriously upset him and he had to sort it out with the Elders. They told him I was the cause of some very serious divisions in the church. He then read a verse from Romans that he said described me.

Romans 16:17-18.... *Now I urge you brethren, keep your eyes on those who cause dissension and hindrances contrary to the teaching which you learned, and turn away from them. For such men are slaves not of our Lord Christ but of their own appetites, and by their smooth and flattering speech, they deceive the hearts of the unsuspecting.*

I had no idea that I was the cause of so much trouble. It should not have been that way. The Elders had overstepped their boundaries by making decisions about people's private lives. On top of that they had gone too far in their methods to gain control over people using intimidation, harassment and now slander. However, being out of the household did not stop the Elders from continuing to pursue Grant and I. Ron called Eileen's place while Stuart and Eileen were at work, saying he wanted to meet with Grant and I right away. Ron was coming over to Eileen's place. We had pledged never to meet with them again so I immediately called Eileen to tell her what was happening. Both Stuart and Eileen left their workplaces to come home and protect us from the Elders. We knew when one said he was coming there would be more and we would be outnumbered.

That is exactly what happened. Stuart and Eileen arrived home just before three Elders knocked on the front door. They were very surprised when Eileen answered and invited them in. She ushered them into the living room. Jeff and Ron sat on a couch opposite and directly facing the couch that Grant and I sat on. Brian sat next to us. Eileen and Stuart sat perpendicular to the rest of us on chairs at either end. Eileen immediately took charge and asked them why they were here. Ron replied saying, "We came to confront these two members of our church with some very grave sins in their lives. Our job is to watch over them and because we love them we want to see them come to repentance."

Eileen said, "If you loved them as you say you do, don't you think you have a responsibility to act in a loving manner towards them? From what I understand from the things that have been going on, it does not sound like you really love them?" She looked at us and said, "Do you think these Elders love you?"

"I don't think so", replied Grant.

I said, "I don't feel like they do."

"You guys know I love you", said Ron.

"No Ron, I don't know that", I countered.

Eileen explained, "When you love someone or bless someone, you don't do it by just saying it. You must actually do something loving or do something to bless them. What I see here is that you just want to accuse and judge these two. That is not what they need right now. They need to be listened to and accepted, not told they are full of sin. Furthermore how can you come in here and accuse them of sin, that is not your job. It is God's place to judge all our hearts and only He can judge correctly."

Eileen carried on and asked them about their motives and she lectured them about how they had hurt us. She supported us by telling Ron, Jeff and Brian why what they were doing was wrong. Eileen's words made me feel wonderful. It was the first time someone had defended us. Eileen went on to speak and showed her depth of understanding on spiritual matters and her wisdom. I could not remember the details of what she said but I felt that Grant, Eileen and I were united in spirit and that she was inspired to say what she said. It was as if the Holy Spirit was speaking to the Elders through her, chastising them. It seemed that God Himself was trying to get through to them. The Elders were visibly shaken by her words.

When Eileen had finished speaking, one of the elders commented, "That is all well and good Eileen, however we cannot accept what you have been saying. If your husband Stuart, had taken his proper place as the head of the household and addressed us instead, we might have listened."

I could not believe what was just said. God Himself had inspired Eileen and she spoke the truth beautifully. These men had rejected those words just because they were delivered by a woman. I could not hold back any longer and I called that Elder an Ass. I told Ron I would come one Sunday morning to the Teaching and confront everyone about what was going on so that we could clear the air. Ron threatened me by saying, "If you dare to try and pull that stunt, I will have you physically thrown out."

I realized that the pain and difficulties with the other members of our church were part of the Elders plan. Having all your friends and those you consider family turn against you, tell you that you are a terrible person and put pressure on you to change your behaviour, was the most brutal form of coercion. The Elders were well aware of this and had instigated it to control us, punish us and destroy our credibility so no one would listen to our concerns. I am not so sure that they even cared if we repented and obeyed them anymore. This was about revenge. Their tactics were aggressive and offensive. They were diligent and cruel. We left the church after this meeting but their attempts to control us, and their pursuit of us, continued long after we had removed ourselves from UBS.

CHAPTER SEVENTEEN

Shortly after I left the UBS household and the church, Donna left the same household with Kari and Beth. She did not want to be there without me. She too left the church, eventually. Donna kept in touch with Grant and I during that period and afterwards. We spent many hours together trying to process what happened to us there. Grant believed UBS was a cult. Donna felt they were scripturally sound but had gone off track with too much power and legalism. I thought they were a good example of the Pharisees in the *Bible* who had abused their power and authority. We were all hurting, feeling a bit lost, rejected and angry. I wanted an apology but none was ever offered and no amends were ever made.

Throughout the following months many questions still haunted me. The wedding plans continued as planned. Grant did most of the work because as much as I wanted this marriage, I felt lethargic and empty. Even the smallest decision was a big deal. My heart and soul continued to wrestle with the old UBS mindset, my new knowing and the freedom to think for myself. There was still a lot of garbage planted in my mind that had to be rooted out without losing my faith in the process. I felt ashamed that I allowed those people to possess me. I had lost myself. My freedom had been stolen from me and I did not know who I was for a time. The magnitude of what happened to me was something more terrifying than anything else I could ever imagine.

The emotional effects were devastating for Grant as well. The Elders had continuously hounded him about his shortcomings. They even tried to convince him that he wasn't really a Christian and had not been saved after all because they did not approve of his behaviour. On many occasions the Elders caused him to doubt his faith and more than once, they had caused him to break down in tears. If he bought someone a gift, they said he was irresponsible and could not handle money properly. If he did not give freely, they said he was selfish. He could not win. Over and over he was told that he had to submit to their authority. However, he refused to give up his own dreams and own identity. He told me "I will not let them make a robot out of me". Over time, I watched the Grant I loved, change from a happy carefree man to a suspicious and withdrawn individual.

By January 1983, I had come to a number of solid conclusions. I started to write down the results of my mental wanderings and flipping so I could have something to hang on to. I believed that the Elders were in fact punishing Grant and I for our disobedience to them. The counsel that they gave us was not really counsel in the true sense. When you counsel someone you listen to them and help them sort things out on their own. You support them with insights. The Elders never listened, they judged, intimidated and controlled. They also had an agenda that did not include our welfare, but that of the church and its goals. True counselling is meant to be based in love and to help someone, not use them so you can help yourself. This was the opposite of counselling. What the Elders did was the opposite of love.

I knew that I was the only one responsible for me. I was the only one who could answer for myself, before God. I was the most important person that needed to love me. I had to follow my heart and have the confidence that I was on the right track. If my own heart did not condemn me, I was good. God gave each of us a mind of our own to use for a reason. I could not let the Elder's lack of peace be the final word but should consider what they said, according to Robert. The unity at all costs within the church is a questionable objective. If you don't know what to do and go along with the Elder's advice that might be OK. However, if you do know what to do and have heard God's message, loud and clear, then ditching that knowledge and taking the Elder's advice instead, is not OK.

In UBS, my understanding of life, of God, of who I was, where I was going and what I should be doing was all arranged into a simple package, rationalized by scripture. The framework had been carefully set up and taught by the Elders through a series of lectures. Those Teachings were the same throughout all the sister churches. There was a lecture on every aspect of life so that how to speak, act and behave was described. For every member of the church these Teachings were received, repeated, reinforced, corrected and enforced when necessary. Each one of us had to agree, obey and behave as expected because this unity, the source of the church's power, was more important than any one person.

The UBS program created a forced, artificial sense of unity with comforting camaraderie and security. Life in UBS was easy, predictable and controlled where everyone had a role in the established hierarchy. Then within this even one's own personal accountability was delegated to those higher up. Therefore the sense of responsibility for one's own choices was no longer burdensome. Decisions did not require thinking because the program supplied all the answers. Experiential learning was limited because the insights from life lessons were interpreted for you. In UBS my ability to perceive and analyze was hampered while my talents for judgmentalism and self righteousness had been heightened. The world in UBS had become black and white. Inside UBS was safe but outside was a place to be feared. All shades of grey were eliminated and shadows were not to be trusted.

Just like the law abiding, authority respecting citizen in the psychology experiment, I no longer had to be personally responsible for what I did. Firmly seated in the UBS framework of thinking, I could very easily detach myself from my own sensibilities, desires and will. I no longer had to think or worry, just simply obey an alien system of standards dictated to me by the authorities responsible for me. Not my decision, not my rules, therefore not my fault. This framework could become destructive and dangerous. Without love for ourselves and others as the controlling and deciding factor in our decision making, we lose our humanity. We become more like robots controlled by computers operating on a binary system of ones and zeros, on and off, black and white.

Knowing these things was a ray of light on my path forward. However the devil was in the details, literally. I was now responsible to re-evaluate everything the Elders and UBS had been telling me. The hard part was differentiating what parts of my system of thinking were mine and what parts were planted there by others. I did not always know when I was being controlled or how. Often I was being pulled in two separate directions of thought. I could not always recognize my own organic voice. I was often confused and distressed even though the spark in me had been ignited.

I had to learn to distinguish truth from lies without throwing away my faith and belief in Christ. It was like having two competing voices in my head. The anchor that kept me from losing my mind was that in my new world, love for myself and others would trump the UBS dos and don'ts. Whenever I was unsure of what to do, I would just evaluate how love is described in the *Bible*. It does not seek its own best interests, puts the needs of others first and always believes the best in others. I then would ask myself what a loving person would do? What is love calling me to do? Armed with this strategy, I would eventually replace the UBS decision making with love. In the end, it would be love that would find me in the mess and teach me who I was all over again.

A few of our friends from UBS had accepted our decision to get married. There were many from the church that I still cared about and missed. Even though reconciliation with UBS was not possible, I was hoping to reclaim a few of my friends. Therefore I sent out invitations to our wedding to many UBSers. Donna was asked to be one of my bridesmaids and agreed but was flipping back and forth. One minute she was for us, the next against. She was having difficulty hanging on the the light of her new found realizations. Without talking to me on a regular basis she would get pulled back into the UBS mindset. She did not have the support I had. Keeping her sane was draining on me, when I was struggling with my own mind. Sadly Donna finally bailed on me, dropped out of the wedding party and reverted to a position of non-support.

Grant's best man was his real life brother who had joined UBS after Grant. He was one of the newer members of UBS and had been in the same household as Grant. He too was also under the supervision of Jason. Jason had initially supported us but as word of our sinful natures spread far and wide, many who said they would attend changed their minds. Jason and his wife eventually decided to boycott our wedding. Grant's best man, his own blood brother and family, also bailed on him. That was painful. Grant had to do a lot of scrambling to find a last minute replacement. Then to top it off, the UBS church organized a fundraising garage sale on the same day and at the same time as our wedding. That gave many more confirmed participants an excuse not to show up.

No matter what happened we forged ahead. We had marriage classes with a local minister. Then we were married in that United Church on May 14, 1983. The wedding was beautiful. I wore a traditional white gown that my mother helped me pick out back home. There were lots of flowers and everything was pink, white and red. One of the musicians in the church had helped Grant write a song for me. Part way through the service it was performed on an electric piano and a guitar to surprise me. I loved it. The weather was cloudy all day but when the service was over and we emerged from the church, the sun shone brilliantly until nightfall.

Both Grant and my family were there. I had two bridesmaids, my sister and a friend from back home. Grant found a UBSer to be his best man. Grant's mother, sister and other brother, not in UBS, were there and so were my parents and many of my aunts and uncles. Of course Eileen, Stuart and the children were there as well. The party afterwards was for a smaller group of invitees where we had a lovely meal of Chicken Cordon Bleu, in a private area of the restaurant. However, between the church and the party venue, Grant and I took off to a nearby tourist area in a baby blue antique car. We went into an eating establishment in an old mill, me in my wedding gown, and had a drink of champagne as we overlooked the scenic waterfall. It was perfect.

There were lots of people supporting us that day and the absentee UBSers, who said they were coming and did not show up, were not really missed. None of the Elders were there but Ron's wife came. I suspected that Ron did secretly support us but had to be united with the other two Elders. We did attend a few UBS Sunday services after we were married but not for long. The negative feelings towards us were still there. Even the well intentioned folks were still trying to save us with advice and correction.

No matter how well things were going for us, the UBSers wanted to believe the worst. It was as if they were looking for proof that the Elders were right. I think they needed us to fail, to reaffirm that their faith in their church and their Elders was correct. We often saw these folks on campus and to and from work. Many were reaching out to us, calling us and making appointments for lunch. However, each encounter was the same. It was just another attempt to reform us and report back to the church, everything that was happening in our lives. These attitudes towards us and the need to always be on the defensive was harmful for us. It was hard not to feel bad about one's self when everyone was constantly telling you that you were bad. To protect our mental health, we had to cut off contact with many of these former friends.

There were, however, a few people we did still trust. We had one such dear friend come over to see our apartment. He looked startled when he walked in. He explained that he expected us to be living in squalor and was surprised how nice our home was. He seemed unusually tense and artificial in his conversation with us. He finally asked us how the marriage was going. We said other than the occasional argument, we loved marriage and were very happy. He questioned us about having a disagreement. He commented that, "...if this was a marriage made in heaven, there would be no arguments." Then he suggested that should never have been married.

I paused for a moment and then said, "I see we have an enemy in our presence." He told us that he was instructed to speak to the Elders before seeing us alone. He said that the Elders had warned him about us and they coached him on how to deal with us. He then told Grant about sins he saw in Grant's life and gave him advice for correction. He also gave us a tape of spiritual music. He finally said he would pray for us and then he left. This was extremely unsettling for us. For a long time we were distraught by this betrayal and loss of yet another friend. The need to change what we were doing and to further distance ourselves from these people, became clearer that day.

The last time I saw the UBS Elders was approximately three months after our wedding. I came across Brian and Jeff sitting outside the Student Union Building. Ron was no longer with them. I was told that Ron and his family packed up and moved to one of the sister churches in the United States. This seemed rather sudden and I wondered if this had anything to do with Grant and I. I had been blamed for causing a split in the church, was that it? I really did not know.

In addition to all the emotional and mental issues, I wanted to know what went wrong with UBS. I needed to know how such a thing like this could happen and how a church could go so wrong. So when I saw the two Elders, I could not resist asking the one burning question that had been haunting me. I went over to the cannon where they were sitting and insisted that I needed to speak with them. They reluctantly sat on the grass away from the ear shot of others.

I asked them, "If you, the Elders, had prayed about something concerning a church member's life, would your answer to that prayer be God's will for that person's life?"

Jeff replied, "Yes."

I then asked, "Would a church member be unwise to go

against the Elders' decision in that situation?"

Again Jeff replied, "Yes."

I went on to ask, "Would that person be committing a sin in that case?"

Jeff again agreed and said that this was correct. He then looked away to show he was getting bored by my questions.

So I summarized the responses by saying, "Does this mean that if a church member does not do what an Elder says, he is in sin. So that a church member, if he wants to be right with God, has no real choice but to do whatever the Elders tell him to do?"

Jeff became impatient and somewhat agitated as he looked across the lawn to an approaching student and said, "Yes, in reality that is right."

I just wanted to be sure about what I had been hearing and I wanted to hear it plainly and directly from these Elder's mouths. I was angry. I retorted, "It is not acceptable for you to have that kind of authority. You cannot speak for God and dictate God's will for others. You are setting yourselves up as God. This wrong thinking will lead your church astray and this is a very serious wrong."

Jeff was silent for a second and very uncomfortable with my loud outburst. In the middle of that statement, Jeff tried to introduce me to the student that had now arrived in our circle. I was not going to be distracted and finished what I had to say. Jeff was embarrassed because the student had heard me. Jeff then turned to me and quietly said, "We do not want to see you ever return to UBS". Then he turned his back on me and picked up a conversation with the student.

197

My concerns with UBS were many. This dictatorship within the church and the lack of transparency surrounding the hierarchical structure was problematic. Now I knew that this was not just a misunderstanding on my behalf. The Elders knew exactly what they were doing and what kind of power they wielded. Faith in God or Christ was replaced by faith in the Elders. They taught that their church was better than all the others. They were right and all other churches had lost their way. This set up a judgmental and self righteous attitude towards others. The narrow interpretation of scripture and strict conformity did not allow for personal expression. This fostered legalistic dogma where decisions, actions and behaviours were rule based instead of being rooted in love.

The roles of men and women as both singles and in a marriage were demeaning to women. Women were encouraged to be submissive and were considered lesser-than the men in every way. Women could only teach other women and had to wear head coverings at prayer meetings and communion (Breaking of Bread). I believe women were preyed upon within the process of forming marriages. The man had to ask first, the Elders would decree it and the woman had no choice but to accept whatever offer of marriage came their way. She could say no but if the Elders said it was God's will, would her refusal mean she was wrong and in sin?

Once in the marriage, the man was the head and made the decisions. The women were expected to bear lots of children and keep the home functioning, so men could be free to seek their self-actualized lives. The children were disciplined with the rod, as often as needed and as hard as required to break their will. This was done in private and strictly hidden. Once the couple had paid any debts, tithing for married couples was ten percent of their salaries or more. I received a pamphlet indicating that ten percent was expected but was told that amount was considered a pittance. Many gave the church all their assets, businesses, homes and cars. None of the church monies went to charities outside the church.

The church used the status of a student club to avoid paying for a building, yet they had money. I once saw them collect ten thousand dollars in two days, from the congregation, for some need in a sister church. The relationship of the church to the greater circle of churches was not made apparent to anyone on the outside. Every church had a different name, so the connections could not be readily made. The church acted independently of all other related churches with no documented, formal oversight. It was run by Elders, acting as trained ministers who had no formal training. UBS operated without any of the checks and balances of mainstream churches. It was this lack of accountability, the blatant lack of transparency and the overt predatory nature and gross power inequities, that had a devastating impact on the lives of many. Not just Grant and I.

Diary late 1983: The techniques of mind control are simply forms of deceitfulness. The tactics include endless repetitive questioning, nitpicking and breaking down the big picture into fragments. Then emphasizing and focusing on the little pieces so that the correct perspective in context is lost and the person becomes confused. The opponent dictates and assumes a position of authority and then mocks and belittles the victim. Treating them like a child and using off-handed comments, causes the victim to lose their self confidence. The perpetrator then uses false logic, pseudo reasoning and half truths to walk the victim through a maze of logic that makes sense, but in reality is a false narrative. The new logic is established, reinforced and then enforced by groups using repetition, guilt and peer pressure in a selected, controlled circle of people.

I continued to mourn the loss of all my friends for a long time. I wondered who else had been hurt by UBS. I remembered seeing Chad standing outside the doors of the Sunday morning Teaching, just months after I started attending UBS Sunday Teachings. He was a tall handsome man, with light coloured hair, in his mid to late twenties and he was crying. He had lived in Jeff's household and had been with UBS for many years. I had heard that he was having a disagreement with the Elders about dating. I never saw him again after that. My heart went out to him as I recalled this event. I now felt I understood what had happened to him and how he must have been feeling. In my soul searching I asked God many questions. As I wrote in my journals, God answered those questions.

Four Questions & Four Answers - October 27, 1983

Question 1: Dear Lord, How could people who are considered Godly, be so wrong about Your will?

Answer 1: I didn't promise you an easy road. I love you and you are special to me and I have a plan for you. You are my child and you do know Me. I want you to learn to be confident in that. Stop leaning on others and do not let anyone confuse you. That is Satan's work. Do not let anyone despise your youthfulness, you can know me just as well as anyone else if you open your heart to Me. It is those that are like children and trust me for all aspects of their life that will enter My Kingdom.

My followers are always striving for maturity in knowing Me by doing the things that will make you more able and capable, more self- sufficient. I don't want you to do that. Striving causes strife, its root word. Sometimes the path is the opposite of what it seems. I want you to become more dependent, not independent, more dependent on Me. I want you to realize more of your weaknesses because in your weakness I can make you strong. It is the least among you who I can use because they require My strength and not their own.

I would never leave you or forsake you ever. Wherever you go I am with you. Like I said, I didn't say My will would be the easy route. It is through the rough road that I will perfect you and show you that I can be trusted.

Yes, sometimes even my followers stand in My way. However, that is not an accident. I have control of all things and I've allowed this for your learning. Don't blame them and don't be angry with them. I love them too. Yes, even My own followers are doing Satan's work. Why not? Just because you are My child doesn't mean you are immune to the schemes of the devil. I have still given you the freedom to choose My way and My commandments, or not. It makes Me happy when I see my children walking in the truth because I know they have chosen this path because they love Me.

You must be careful to do all things in love, righteousness and truth. That means whatever you do, do it because of love and according to the right motives, and because you know it will please Me. Doing things in truth means you do not fool yourself into thinking you are choosing a right motive in order to justify your real reasons for doing something. Know the honest and accurate condition of your heart, the truth of your heart in doing a deed. Be careful, do not deceive yourself. I am not mocked for whatsoever a man sows he will also reap.

Sometimes My followers hurt people because they think they are doing a good thing but it is not done in love. Please above everything else, love Me with all your heart and your neighbour as yourself. My commandment is to love one another. It is not until you do this that all My other words to you will fall into the proper perspective. Please do not love with just word and tongue but in deed

201

and truth.

I have given you the Holy Spirit to teach you and guide you in all these things according to My will. In this way I can be a part of you. So please listen to my still small voice inside of you.

****

Question 2: *Dear Lord, Why was I so afraid to leave the church?*

Answer 2: *I would never leave you. I am with you always, even to the ends of the earth. You are my child and I will guide you with My righteous right hand. Even if you make your bed in Sheol, I am there. Fear is not from Me for I am love and perfect love casts out fear. Do not be afraid, have faith in Me and the things I have shown you. I am in the church and outside the church. I am everywhere. I am the One who will perfect the work I started with you. I am the One who makes you stand. The church cannot do that and neither can you. Have faith in Me and not in man or in works or in churches. These things cannot help you be more like Me.*

There are many other flocks who love Me and I have a place for you. Put away your pride and vanity and stop judging My children in other churches. Your judgment of them makes it difficult for Me to teach you because you are relying on your own understanding. You stick to the things you already know and will not accept anything else. Please listen and hear My voice. Do not harden your heart.

How can I use you for My work if you are afraid? Please don't let fear stop you or hinder you from doing what I ask. I love you and there is no need to be afraid. I am with you and I am your God. Do not be afraid to love others either. If you love others as I love you, you will understand and forgive them when they try to hurt you.

****

Question 3: *Dear Lord, Why is it that so many non-believers have their lives more together and are better living people than followers devoted to You?*

Answer 3: *You are my child and you are a new follower. I adopted you and I am teaching you but you are not perfect yet. You know that I died for you and washed you as clean as snow when you believed in Me. However, you still get tarnished now and then and I will continue to wash you if you come to Me and allow Me to. There are still lots of areas of your life that collect dirt.*

Don't be deceived by outward appearances of people who keep the law and appear to do everything right. This definition of religious life is not necessarily Mine and is not what I want. Your idea of the perfect follower may not be Mine, but as you get to know me you will understand more of My concepts.

I desire a humble and contrite heart that loves Me and their fellow followers. People may appear to be outwardly good but I look at the heart and only I can rightly judge people's hearts. It is only your faith in Me that justifies you, not your abilities to act according to man's standards of what a good person or church is supposed to be. Remember that this is only the start of your walk with Me. There is work to do with you and we have an eternity together to do it.

My desire is for all to come to know Me, find My peace and experience My forgiveness and salvation. You can help Me by keeping My commandment which is to love Me, love yourself and love others. This judging will keep you from loving them because part of loving is accepting

203

people where they are. To Me all of My creation is precious to Me and you are all equal. Please share with others My love and show them that I care for them by your actions.

****

Question 4: *Dear Lord, Why could the Elders not hear me when I tried to tell them where I was at?*

Answer 4: *Do you remember what you read about the problems I had communicating with the Pharisees? They wanted to know where I got the authority to say the things that I said. I didn't fit their idea of what a godly man should be. ...and I didn't do all the things I was supposed to do to prove to them that I was holy and pure. They judged Me according to their own rules and understanding that they worshiped and refused to question. Their judgment of Me blinded them from seeing the truth. In their eyes My witness or example was invalid because of My outward appearance and actions. They were not able to see Me as I was because they saw Me as they thought I was...*

Rules crafted by men who do not know Me, seldom apply. The strict adherence to laws, legalism, is from Satan and oppresses people. It keeps them in bondage and doesn't allow them the freedom to do what I ask. Put away your rules, your religion and your mindset and listen to Me. Don't let legalism hinder you from discovering Me in greater ways that you or any church you ever imagine.

The Elders looked at your actions and interpreted them as being rebellious without ever knowing your heart... They were convinced of their own understanding and were blinded to the truth... you had become invalid in their eyes...I know your heart and you have confessed your sins. You are forgiven. Don't let anyone condemn you. Satan is

*the accuser of my followers and you need to know it is not
from Me. Please let love be your guide in everything. No
rules or code of ethics or religious standards ever count.
The only thing that counts is faith expressing itself through
love.*

*...Try to practise what you have learned. Don't hurt
others but love them as I love you, unconditionally. Love
them no matter what they do to you. Trust me because I
care for all My children. Forgive them for in your
forgiveness you will be totally healed.*

Grant and I were both in desperate need of healing. The
church debacle had taken its toll on the both of us. I was
becoming increasingly withdrawn and Grant was angry.
We were both having difficulty making new friends and
were suspicious of everyone we met. We became a bit
paranoid, thinking each encounter with a stranger might be
a spy. I also did not want new friends knowing about my
past with the church. I knew that the healing would be a
long term project and some scars would always remain.
The continued actions of the Elders were intended to make
their predictions come true, by inserting as many stumbling
blocks in our way as possible. For the sake of our sanity
we stopped having any contact with anyone associated
with UBS.

We obtained an unlisted phone number. We eventually
had to move to a new apartment where we refused to give
out the address to anyone except Eileen, Stuart and my
family, but not Grant's. The hard part was keeping our
location a secret from Grant's brother who was still a
UBSer. To do this we could not tell Grant's own mother
where we lived. We lived like this, incognito, for many
months. It took almost this long before I was comfortable
meeting new people. When my father had a heart attack,
both of us pulled up our shallow roots and moved to where
I grew up, to start over. That move helped improve our

well being tremendously but the larger healing required many more years after that.

Grant and I had the average newlywed arguments but on top of this we were also burdened with sorting out the emotional damage and wrong thinking. We had to help each other free our minds from the programming, which is a very difficult thing to do. I was trying to hide my UBS self that would emerge at the wrong time. All of a sudden I would flip and find myself standing on a pedestal and being very judgy with others. Then I had to walk myself back to discover what I was thinking to react that way. Often it would take days of searching my heart, my mind and reeducating myself to flip back to the normal me mode. It was exhausting and not conducive to the state of mind that welcomed a social life. I preferred to be alone for many years.

Grant had to go through the same process. We supported each other in doing this the best we could. If we had a disagreement, we had to calm down, communicate intensively and sort out what was said to identify the religious dogma. Once we labelled it, we would decide together how valid that thinking was in our new normal. That wrong thinking would be categorized and given a name to help us see it, if one of us slipped into using it. We would call out the name of that piece of dogma to warn the other what had happened. As time went on, Grant and I became better and quicker at recognizing the UBS thinking. It had a specific character and flavour. Eventually we were able to intercept the program before it could interfere with our own thoughts. It took four years of personal and joint self-deprogramming to get to that point in our recoveries.

CHAPTER EIGHTEEN

By 1986, I could see the errors in the mindset I had been taught by UBS, however I continued to explore why it happened. I wanted to understand the root cause. I learned that what happened to UBS, can happen to any group or organization under the wrong conditions. The coercion, manipulation and control with which UBS managed their flock, was done using methods of mind control that play on the basic conditions of human nature.

The Elders laid out a very appealing program of what they were about and they advertised superior knowledge and insight into the scriptures. They presented a fairly simple protocol for members to follow based on chosen scriptures. The established members did not question the protocols and new members, experiencing the social pressure to fit in and be accepted, were inhibited from asking questions.

This need, coupled with the established members' disapproval of any dissension or flexibility in the interpretation of scripture, added another level of intimidation. The group pressure to be united and seek friendships within the group and the confusion that sameness is the same as unity, effectively suppressed individuality. That sameness extended beyond morals and ethics but also seeped into lifestyle and personal choices. The high level of uniformity in all areas of life, with a tight knit group, provides a warm and fuzzy good feeling of security that all humans crave.

As the circle of contacts becomes smaller and tighter, any diversity threatens that feeling of security. In such an environment, an us versus them attitude develops quickly. Then as the walls and boundaries get thicker, tighter, information and contacts from the outside world becomes less and filtered. Being able to make unbiased decisions becomes impossible. In this way the Elders used the established members to exert a large amount of control over the newcomer. Then the Elders controlled what and when information was supplied to the flock. In such a group a person's ability to make choices is restricted.

A person ensnared in this way is easily manipulated and made powerless using knowledge, guilt and correction disguised as instruction, to destroy the person's self-confidence. Elders are now not just teachers but judges that speak for God to whom the new member is now accountable. The secret rules and true agenda then become enforceable, with someone who would never have accepted such conditions and expectations in the beginning.

This can happen in any organization that becomes ingrown in this way and that gives too much authority to too few, without adequate checks and balances to make the leaders accountable. In the religious world, there are additional variables that can contribute to the development of cult-like behaviour. Harold Bussell in his book *Unholy Devotion*, explains how errors in the Christian religious thinking can foster manipulative and abusive situations.

For example he mentions that attractive churches with

dynamic leaders can sometimes give the impression of spirituality. Spiritual talk and lingo used by some Christians can be deceptive and hide what a person really says or believes. Sometimes when someone says, for example, that they are acting on God's directions, they may be just using this statement to justify and avoid taking responsibility for what they are really doing.

This generation wants everything now and they want to fast track their path to Christian maturity. Churches that offer simple answers and tangible results, that they can talk about to demonstrate their faith, are appealing. Some churches even teach that it is possible to live a sin free life. Bussell says, "We were not called to witness to spiritual perfection but to a need for God's grace. We are not called to have great faith in God but faith in a great God."

The dangers of establishing the belief that we can become holy or sinless, sets the stage for infallible leaders to dominate the flock. Church members can let pastors and ministers take the place of Christ. God will judge us individually no matter what our leaders have told us to do. Our pastors will not be judged in place of us if we obey them. True and good leaders are humble enough to admit their fallibility and set a good example for others. They would also not try and control others or force their ideas or beliefs on them. Good leaders support and encourage, not judge and criticize. Bussell says the Greek word for authority (exousia) in the *New Testament*, "...does not imply any jurisdiction over other people's lives. It implies the authority of truth, wisdom and experience of a leader held up as a special example."

Some churches tend to regard ministry oriented careers as being better in terms of one's service to God. They believe that religious vocations have a higher calling than secular careers. First of all, the splitting of one's life into spiritual versus secular is problematic and unhealthy. Our lives need to be continuous and whole throughout the spectrum. Secondly, God asks us to live our lives as Christ would want us to, in everything we do, no matter what we do.

The other problem in Christian teaching is legalism. This is discussed in the book of Galatians in the *New Testament*. Paul wrote about the evils of legalism which occurs when people make up rules and regulate their lives according to these rules, that may have very little to do with what Christ has asked of us. Jesus came to set us free and the *Old Testament* commandments have been written in our hearts. In the *New Testament,* the Spirit within us helps us fulfill those laws when we love God, ourselves and each other. When we follow the one commandment to love, all the other laws fall in behind as God gives us the grace to do good.

Legalism is the reverse of this where the laws and rules come first, sometimes without looking to God for grace or loving. Deeds done in this way may appear to be good according to the laws but the motives and attitude of the heart may not be. The rules can be used to measure one's spirituality and to judge others. The rules also set standards which we can use to decide who to accept and who to reject. The rules also help us to go through the motions of what Christ expects, without examining our true motive and our hearts. They also help us to hide and avoid responsibility for what we are truly doing. It fosters self righteousness, pride and we can end up worshipping the created laws and religion instead of our Creator.

In July 1986, I began to think of legalism as one of the root causes and core issues with what happened in UBS. In Saint Catherine of Sienna's *Treatise on Discretion*, from *A Dialogue with God,* I understood from her that the key was to learn humility, self-knowledge, love God and the virtues first. The root errors in our faith come when we put penance first. If we reverse these two everything else we do becomes tainted and spoiled. I understood the penance could be correlated to all the religious activities we do. I also took this to mean that we are to love God and love the good, not the doing of the good that is important. Later I wrote:

> *Fundamental extremists lay down the absolute interpretation of scripture as laws to be diligently enforced. This outward obedience allows seeds of evil to flourish in unsupervised hearts. Busyness with doing good and conforming with standards leaves little time or motivation to pursue one's own unique path in life. The laws, judgments and standards paint blinders on the window of life and all that God is. Prophets tell us to turn from our evil ways and worship the true and caring God. However in doing that, we then gravitate towards more subtle and deforming evils that a legalistic religion encourages. Intolerance of those who are different, cutting off of those we label sinners, self-righteous attitudes based on our abilities to outwardly conform and fear of the world around us. All these things threaten our purity of heart.*

In *Unholy Devotion*, Ronald Enroth is quoted as saying, "In strongly authoritarian movements or churches, those who persist in raising uncomfortable questions, especially after they have left the group, are labelled reprobates and worse yet, agents of Satan. The weak and meek who have legitimate concerns and questions, do not dare to share those reservations, sometimes because of group pressure, sometimes because they have been subjected to control mechanisms of fear, guilt and spiritual intimidation."

This research into the root causes of what went wrong in UBS, helped me understand what happened to us. It helped me lift the blame and shame I was feeling about allowing these people to possess me like that. Looking back, I can now see that this could have happened to anyone because of the systemic triggers that were allowed and put in place to intentionally trap newcomers. It was not my fault and I have nothing to be ashamed of. I was lucky that I was able to leave and I credit Grant for sticking with me, through his pain and Eileen and Stuart for supporting us. Without them, as strong-willed and confident as I am and have always been, I may have never left. Many friends of mine did not escape.

The loss of all those people I left behind saddened me but I no longer grieved those losses. The final and complete healing began when I had truly and sincerely learned to love and accept people who were very different from me. I learned to set aside my program of judgment and appreciate people for who they are. My world was no longer divided between Christian and heathen. I could now see that God was working in everyone of all faiths, religions and spiritual practices.

I had rediscovered my own identity, the best one can. I was able to speak, behave and interact with people unhindered from the UBS program and the rules and expectations of others. No more flipping. I also studied theology and the lives of the saints. In taking the blinders off, I challenged the misinformation about the Roman Catholic church I had been taught, by studying that faith. In the process I fell in love with the wisdom I saw there.

The memory of UBS and the friends I left behind would motivate me to tell my story and warn others. In 1987 I wrote to the *Cult Project* in Montreal to see if their organization was aware of UBS. This group contributes to and is part of an educational, cult awareness, news network. I also wanted to know if they had any information about the UBS international conglomerate headquarters known as *The Great Commission Church*. In response I was sent one article written by a woman who had an unpleasant experience with one of the sister churches in the

212

United States. I was also given a second piece of information that described the purchase of a radio station by one of the UBS founders and his pro-Contra political sympathies. The *Cult Project* suggested to me that I should put my experiences down in writing. That is when I started thinking about this book.

I did not own a personal computer and at that time, it was not common for everyone to have one. I was working full time, had a two year old and another child on the way. I penned most, if not all, of the first copy of this book in journals while on the bus while travelling to and from work. I had collected many resources, my diaries, magazine articles from my time in the church and used that as reference material. It took two and a half years to write this by hand.

Eventually I had to put everything on a computer to be properly printed. I took three weeks of vacation time from my work, as a laboratory assistant, and sat at one of the terminals in the basement of the computer science lab of our university. I typed like a mad woman every day for eight hours. Then I would leave to pick up my son from daycare where together we travelled one hour back home, by bus. This was the only chance I would get that year. Otherwise I would have to wait for next year's vacation time. The result was a collection of 5.25 inch floppy disks containing the original version. My heart longed for justice and this was the motivation that kept me writing.

At mass on Sunday morning, October 22, 1989, the priest spoke about God's love for us and how He would not withhold justice from those that asked. He was our Father and justice would be satisfied quickly if we petitioned Him. The priest read from Luke 18:1-8.

...And the Lord said, You notice what the unjust judge has to say? Now will not God see justice done to His

chosen who cry to Him day and night even when He delays
to help them? I promise you, he will see justice done to
them, and done speedily...

At that moment I said a prayer. I directed that longing in my heart to God, to ask for justice for those who had been hurt by UBS. I meditated and reflected on all my former friends who were left behind, Kari, Beth, Donna and many others, the deeds of this church and I committed this request to God. That evening I had to go to the lab to prepare for an early morning experiment. My son was with me and I was listening to the CBC radio. At five o'clock, just as I was gathering my things to leave, the national news came on. The news stunned me. This was about the church that had harmed Grant and I. This was the UBS I wrote about. It was really the University Bible Studies but I referred to it at the University Bible School, in my story. They had reported the following statement that was issued by the Public Relations office of the University of Guelph dated September 13, 1989:

The University of Guelph Central Student Association
has removed University of Guelph Bible Studies from its
list of approved student clubs and the University of Guelph
has prohibited the group from conducting club activities
on campus.

This action was taken following allegations that some
club activities were contradictory to the values of the
university. These concerns and other information
regarding the club were reviewed by a group of University
of Guelph students and administrators. The group
concluded that allegations of coercive proselytization,
authoritarianism and subservience of women were real,
that these activities had persisted over several years
despite discussions with student and staff representatives
and that they were a serious affront to individual rights
and the university's values.

This decision reinforces the university's commitment to provide a learning environment in which students are free to develop themselves intellectually, spiritually and personally, without being subject to controlling authoritarian practices.

From what I understood based on my research, COMA, the Committee on Mind Abuse, in Toronto was called to carry out an investigation of UBS and the *Great Commission Church*, in response to complaints. UBS, now called Grace Community Church, were now meeting at a school in Guelph. The results of this investigation was that this group was a Destructive Cult and that membership with this group was not recommended. The Student Judicial Committee had separate complaints of their own that UBS had violated the rules defining student club status. They asked that the club be removed. Then the president of the University of Guelph made a separate decision based on the investigation that was done, additional supporting evidence and the advice of their lawyers and had the club banned.

I also believe that UBS appealed these decisions and the decisions were upheld. There was both a lot of criticism and much support for the university in these rulings. Those who criticized the university felt they were heavy handed and intolerant of diversity and religious rights. From my perspective, this was long overdue and a prudent decision based on good judgment and valid information. The University of Guelph student newspaper, the *Ontarion*, published this statement on October 10, 1989: "We, the Campus Ministers at the university of Guelph, were consulted and agree with the position of the university regarding the University Bible Studies Club..."

The Guelph newspaper, *The Mercury*, published an article in September 1989 which contained the following quotes from interviews with John Fairchild (named Jeff in my story), one of the pastors (Elders) of UBS.

John Fairchild, the pastor of the Grace Community Church with which the club, UBS is affiliated, says he has not received complaints related to the university charges. "There have been people we disagreed with", Fairchild said, "but that is everyday life."

He said the university report that the Bible club had been kicked off four other university campuses is untrue. He said the club never had a chapter at Ryerson and Waterloo and the two clubs started at York and McMaster were folded voluntarily because of lack of support. "We are looking at this as a procedural blunder that is totally out of character with the university", said Fairchild. He said he would like to see the club have the opportunity to defend itself.

The Kitchener-Waterloo newspaper, *The Record*, published an article by a reporter on staff, Jim Fox, on October 2, 1989 about the University of Guelph and their decision about UBS.

The University of Guelph says it won't reconsider its ouster of the University Bible Studies Club over allegations it conducted cult-like activities on campus. University officials slammed the door on attempts by a lawyer acting for the club who sought a hearing to discuss the allegations. "No meeting will be held and the prohibition will remain in place," R.S. Sleightholm, lawyer for the university said, in a letter to Frank Carere, acting for the club.

The club, which has about thirty members and is affiliated with Grace Community Church, was kicked out of its offices last month after an investigation into complaints. It was concluded that allegations of "coercive proselytization, authoritarianism and subservience of women were real and these activities persisted over several years, despite discussions with student and staff representatives," the university reported. Scott Mohr, the club's campus representative, said members were never contacted or given a chance to have a defence or explain.

Grace Church, which operated the club, "is an independent, evangelical, Bible-believing type of conservative church," said pastor John Fairchild. Their lawyer said the prohibition, "contravenes our client's fundamental freedoms of conscience, religion, expression, peaceful assembly and association." The university's position is that it has the right, as owner of the property, to exclude anyone and the decision does not mean the club cannot continue its activities off campus.

"We don't want anything to do with them," Marty Williams, president of the Central Student Association, said. The association is responsible for monitoring the activity of clubs and accrediting them.

"Since the original investigation, as a result of a complaint from a Windsor area man, whose daughter became involved in the group, other people have come forward to compare the club to a cult," Williams said. The family said they lost all contact with their daughter, who is in her early 20's, after she joined and was forced to marry a member of the club. They said she underwent a dramatic personality change and abandoned her studies to become a recruiter for the group.

Robert Tucker, director of the Toronto based Council on Mind Abuse, said the group displayed all the characteristics of a cult in which leaders gradually impose total, but subtle, control over the members...It was found that the Guelph club and others are affiliated with the Colorado based Great Commission International, which is on about 80 universities in the United States.

The Peak, an alternative student newspaper, published an article called, *Is UBS a Cult?* in its October 5, 1989 publication. It was written by Stephen Parks and I documented some excerpts from that article.

The University Bible Studies was founded in 1972 at Iowa State University by James McCotter. When it started, it was called Alpha Omega, but has since changed its name numerous times. Solid Rock, The New Covenant Christian Fellowship and The Great Commission are just some of the names that it has been known by. When Iowa authorities started investigating McCotter's involvement in a tax evasion scheme, he decided to move to California. He is currently believed to be in Washington D.C. Area, where apparently, UBS is planning a big campaign aimed at high school students. As an Amway salesman and an Apostle in his church, McCotter has been criticized both externally and internally for abusing his position for personal economic gains. In spite of this his group continues to grow...

But is UBS a Cult? Members say no. Ex-members and organizations such as COMA, CFF, AFF say yes. The fact that UBS has changed its name so many times, is rather suspicious. Even here, they were The Great Commission until a year ago. Under its many names, it has run afoul of a few university administrations; Western, McMaster and Ryerson in Canada, and universities in the states of Iowa, Colorado and New York. They have circulated pamphlets such as the *Forty Ways to Discredit the Catholic Church* and freely admit that they believe that they themselves are the one true church. Some of UBS's tactics include circular logic (such as the statement that an Elder's word is the Word of God. Why? Because an Elder said so...). By using this reasoning, no one is allowed to question any Elder's statement.

The Intelligencer, of the Belleville Daily published an article on October 2, 1989, titled *Fundamentalists Work Hard on Campus*. Excerpts about UBS included the following:

...Robert Tucker, director of the Toronto based Council on Mind Abuse, said "the groups preach a rigid style of fundamentalist Christianity, but their methods closely resemble those of a cult. ...It all starts out very friendly", Tucker said in an interview... "New students are invited to a Bible meeting and they meet friends. But soon, they are taken through an assault on their sense of self."

...Barbara Lloyd, a former member of the Great Commission club at Ohio State University, said group leaders gradually impose total, but subtle, control over their members... Lonely and away from home for the first time, she joined the group because it offered friends and a variety of social activities. During the more than five years she was involved, her life included only the group and her education studies. "They stressed loyalty to the leadership with no questions asked. Women were to be very submissive and there was no dating."

When she began asking too many questions, the group arranged for her to marry a member she hardly knew and had never dated. "I thought I was supposed to marry him, even though I have hardly been friends with him. He wasn't my type of guy", she said. ...Lloyd managed to leave the group in February 1987 only after her parents kidnapped her and the family spent one week holed up in a remote cottage with a deprogramming counsellor. She spent a further two weeks at a rehabilitation centre for victims of cults.

While Grant and I spent our years of recovery from UBS, I came into contact with a family from Windsor with a story very much like the one described in the article by *The Record*. I don't know who the family was that launched the complaint but I became very close to the parents of someone who lost their daughter to UBS. We exchanged letters regularly and shared our faith with one another. I was able to describe to them what I had experienced, as a woman of a similar age to their estranged daughter. I grew to love them through our correspondence and was able to help them express their pain and grief. We facilitated each other's healing as they obtained details of my experience to assist them with their own situation. They too supported me in writing this book which I shared with them. Eventually we lost touch and to this day I don't know if they ever got their daughter back.

Five years after leaving UBS, Grant and I were very happy. We had beautiful children, a nice home and a dog in a family friendly neighbourhood, not far from where I went to school as a child. At that time we had a four year old son and a two year old daughter and in the next year, a third daughter on the way. Our ordeal with UBS was in the past, just one of the many trials and struggles that life has to offer. We had many successes, Grant in business and myself in my career in research, which I loved. It was hard to salvage my faith in churches but I was able to find a place. My faith had grown even stronger as I had to learn to trust God for myself.

The members of UBS were afraid for us because they believed God would certainly abandon us. Many years ago, in my past life and at my lowest point in my UBS ordeal, a professor, someone I respected, called me an agent of Satan. I came close to believing that back then. After wandering around town in a daze, I came across a little Pentecostal church. There some people there helped me get my head screwed back on and I recovered as per my story. The Elders back then, had said our marriage would be a disaster, "the worst marriage in the world."

On that calm and quiet Sunday afternoon in 1990, Grant and I were enjoying some leisure time, lying on the bed, playing with the kids. It had been seven years after leaving UBS. Out of the blue Grant turned to me and asked, "Do you think the Elders were right about our getting married?" I smiled and thought for a moment about all the truths I learned, all the light I clung to in those periods of darkness and how I had come to trust that God was always with me. I thought about all the wonderful people I met and the life changing experiences that shaped who I was. God had truly blessed us. I then looked at Grant and our beautiful children, laughing and giggling. I then turned to him, looked into his eyes with certainty and conviction and answered him with my own final proclamation, "No, they were very, very wrong."

EPILOGUE

This story was written seven years after the events occurred. Although much healing had taken place, without a crystal ball, I would not have known that it was still an additional seven years before I could finally feel I had wrestled and defeated that demon from UBS. There were so many last remnants that needed to be uncovered and healed. I learned that I needed to be patient with myself and that I had no control over Grant's healing. I really did not know where he went with it. When UBS was no longer an issue, we never felt the need to discuss it anymore. In the republishing of this in 2006, my best advice was to protect yourself, warn others and prevent these groups from doing the damage that they do.

The story does not end there however. Grant and I did have a good life together. Now in 2021, looking way back, almost forty years, I see I may have underestimated the damage done by UBS. When I met Grant, I fell in love with his self confidence and passion for life. As the years went on over the course of our marriage, Grant worked hard to succeed. However, there was an underlying current where it seemed he needed to prove himself to me, my parents and others. His need to be seen as successful, was a driving force that may have been fuelled by a lack of self worth. Although I upheld him in every way and never criticized him, he felt I was looking down on him. I did have more education and this played on him. I may have contributed to this by being distant, resentful and preoccupied with my own spiritual healing.

Looking back I believe that the UBS experience had scarred us forever. I think UBS broke him at one point and I don't think those wounds ever fully healed. How do you recover from being told you are the worst person ever, an unworthy sinner, by everyone in your life, at a young and impressionable age? After eleven years of marriage, Grant moved on to another family. He became estranged from us and his children. He never had the chance to meet his grandkids. He always said he would die young and he did leave us far too soon at the age of fifty-two.

I will always be grateful to him for loving me and saving me when I needed it the most. He freed my mind to new ideas and new ways of thinking. He was a risk taker that was outside my comfort zone and not in my nature. However, I learned to be courageous and jump into life with more passion. Through Grant's motto to just do it and figure out the details later and my faith as a safety net, I accomplished a great many things that I am proud of. There is no question that the three amazing children that we had together, are people who God wanted to come into this world, through the two of us. I am more convinced today than ever that it was God's will for us to be married, those many years ago.

The cult experience did have an impact on the remaining decades of my life. I became a person in search of the truth, intent on understanding what it meant to be free. I was obsessed with finding out what God really wanted me to do and who I was. After all, I had lost my personality and freedom for a time. That would never happen again. I attacked life with passion and left a wake behind me, stirring up a lot of discontent along the way. Just like the cult experience, my life has continued to be strange and event filled. So much so that I wrote another book about these twists and turns, called *Love's Call to Madness*.

In 2006 I created some tips for protection from becoming a victim, advice on how to help another person leave a damaging group and lessons on what to do after leaving a destructive situation. Today's world has become even more inundated with false news and polarized extremist beliefs. The information in these pages can be applied to many situations and organizations. That was my motivation to publish this to a wider audience in 2021. Then I did a quick Google search about UBS, thinking that I would only find historical references. I was horrified to see that the same international conglomerate of churches still exists and some of the same leaders are still active. What is worse, I found a branch of this church in Toronto, Canada. Arrrggghhh! I pray to God they have changed their ways. If not, this book about an event that took place almost four decades ago, is still apropos for today.

Lessons Learned:

Tips to help you from being victimized by recognizing a damaging group:
- Keep in touch with family and friends and listen when they have concerns about you. Remember they love you and know you best, even if there is tension in the family. They are your reality check
- Note any feelings of inferiority or self doubt when you are with group members. Remember if people really love you, they will respect your opinions even if they differ from the those of the group
- Know why you do things and ask questions. If you do not have an adequate answer other than "you

wouldn't understand" or "we know best", don't do it. The same applies to why you are told you are not allowed to do something

- Ask a lot of questions and challenge the group in a respectful way. Look for signs of anger or agitation in group members, especially leaders. Watch to see if the response turns to personal put downs or attacks on your credibility
- Listen for any comments that indicate intolerance to people outside the group. Loving others means being respectful and tolerant of others
- Note the amount of time you spend with the group. Maintain balance with your friends, family and educational commitments outside the group. Watch for pressure to tip the balance of time towards the group. If the group members really love you, they will want you to be successful in all areas of your life
- Look for signs of secrecy. Do you have trouble finding out about the group membership, leaders and affiliated groups? Is there a public record of the group's mandate, doctrine and finances? What happens when you ask? If the group has nothing to hide, then they should be open about these things
- Look for signs of turmoil between group members that nobody talks about. Is everything always great when you sense something is amiss? Do they never admit to having problems? It is natural and healthy for people to have differences
- Most of all, do not underestimate the power the group has to persuade you. The biggest danger is your own confidence that you can handle them and won't get drawn in. If you try to leave, and they continue to stalk you, despite your objections, this is a good sign that you made the right choice to leave. Get your phone number changed, cut them off on social media and avoid them at all costs

Tips to help somebody else recognize and leave a damaging group:

- Study the group and collect as much research as possible about how they operate and their system of beliefs. You need to know more about the group than the person you are trying to help

- Learn how the group thinks and understand the lingo they use and what that means. The key is knowing how they think and gently and respectfully challenging those thoughts and assumptions

- Get help from an ex-member or expert who knows the group. This is invaluable but don't be caught associating with them. You will lose all credibility with the person you are trying to help because the group would have already discredited all ex-members. They are the enemy

- Do not criticize or judge the group or person you are helping. Appear to be as open as possible and accepting of the group. Listen carefully and agree where you can with the person. Then take one area and gently challenge them. Don't dwell on it but just plant a small seed for them to consider

- Find every opportunity to visit and spend time with this person. Be consistent and show up. Use the same techniques used by the group to lure them. Be kind, pleasant and friendly but instead of counterfeit love offer real love and caring

- Keep the lines of communication open at all costs and challenge the inconsistencies at every opportunity very carefully, without breaking the bond you have developed

- Build up the person's self esteem by reminding them how capable they are. Damaging groups erode members' self esteem to get them to accept the authoritative structure. Shoring up the confidence that has been lost is critical to their ability to leave

- Encourage them to get rest and eat well. Invite them over and let them have a nap and feed them something nourishing. Damaging groups often keep their members stressed and tired so they will give in more easily to pressures to obey
- Teach the person you are trying to help the difference between being nice, pleasant, friendly and real caring. Point out problems with the good deeds the person experiences in the group. For example is a visit from a fellow member with muffins when you are studying for a big exam, really caring given you were in a time crunch?
- Don't get discouraged. You may make some progress only to have the group reinforce and undo everything you had done. Group members consistently keep other members in check. Get support for yourself and keep the vigil going no matter what. Know that your real love and caring will win out in the end. The person you are helping will see that
- Failing any progress or hope that the person will be able to leave on their own. Have the person extracted from the group by professionals. Then carry on all the above tips continuing that bond of caring you already initiated. You may need professional programmers but your role in caring for the person should continue throughout the healing process to keep them from going back to the group

Tips to help you exit a damaging group on your own, if you become ensnared and what to do after you leave:
- The realization that something is wrong will not always be a light-bulb moment but will come to you more like a flickering light. Pay attention to moments of doubt that are recurring and nagging
- Take note of something that has come into this field of realization or perspective. Write it down so

you don't forget it. Daily journaling can help you keep track of your private thoughts without permanently losing them when the group reinforces the old thinking

- When you are ready, get support from a knowledgeable person outside the group that you trust. Do not let the group know about this person and pick someone who is credible and can challenge the group leadership, should you need it. The group will attack this person to make you lose trust in them

- Take a close look at the system of beliefs you have been sold for inconsistencies and errors. Research what you find, gather proof and collect your own evidence to validate your rationale for leaving and support you in your decision

- Do not meet with the leaders alone, if you have been found to be questioning too much. Take your outside support with you, if possible and document everything that is said. Be prepared for an escalation of pressure. They may threaten you and they will criticize you, so be prepared. If possible try and leave before you become noticed and a target

- When you do leave, don't tell anyone you are doing it and do it quickly. Have someone from outside with you in case you are confronted or physically prevented from leaving. Don't underestimate how difficult it is to leave. The group will wear you down and the comfort, support, security and friendship will pull you back into the vortex. It is easier to stay than to face the unknown outside. Take note of this struggle and focus on your future welfare like your life depends on it. It does

- Reestablish friendships on the outside as soon as possible. The loss of the group and the negative rumours they will spread about why you left are certain to start circulating. Find people to support you and do not trust or have contact with anyone from the group

- Get professional help for mental health support and depression. Also find a professional that specializes in deprogramming or exciting groups like the one you were in. You have lost your entire world, friends and purpose in life. It will take time to reclaim those things and replace them
- Give yourself time to grieve, be angry, sad and experience all those emotions and thoughts that the group may have caused you to avoid or suppress. Do not make important life decisions at this time, if possible, until you have adequate time to heal
- Know that random thoughts constantly influence our behaviour and emotions. Force yourself to become aware of these background thoughts. You will periodically flip back into thinking the same way as the group. Take note of these times and how they affected you. Be the detective and root out the incorrect thinking that triggered the event and replace it with new thoughts. Keep track and write these down
- Do not blame yourself for what happened. You are the innocent victim of someone else's failure to respect you and your boundaries. The techniques used by destructive groups are well disguised and effective. This can happen to anyone
- Always be thankful that you left the group. Treasure your freedom. Enjoy discovering your own unique talents, passions and contributions to the world. Use this as one of life's lessons in a positive way and share what you have learned with others

Much love and Blessings,
SG Williams,
June 27, 2021

ABOUT THE AUTHOR

SG Williams has spent decades working in science, research, technology and continuously studying as a life-long learner. It has only been in the last decade she has worked in the public eye as a quasi part-time activist trying to bring peace and wellness to the community.

She believes in simplicity, authenticity, inner peace and keeping the wonder of life alive by paying attention to our surroundings. She sees every person as unique and specially created with something important to teach us. In her opinion it is imperative for everyone to have access to healthy communities, where people can be appreciated for who they are, free from injustice and discrimination.

Now, through her books, she hopes to offer emotional validation for those who are suffering. She hopes that she can be a voice for change or a catalyst for others to speak out, by describing the injustices she sees, experiences and hears through the stories of others.